Robe

Tr

Text adaptation by **Christopher Hall**

Activities by **Adeline Richards**

Illustrated by **Paolo D'Altan**

Editor: Rebecca Raynes
Design and art direction: Nadia Maestri
Computer graphics: Simona Corniola
Picture research: Laura Lagomarsino

First edition : May 2007

Picture credits
The Scottish National Portrait Gallery: 4; Private Collection,
Peter Newark Historical Pictures / The Bridgeman Art
Library: 31, 33, 59; Topham Picturepoint TopFoto.co.uk: 35,
93; The Granger Collection, New York: 61; Mary Evans
Picture Library: 86, 89, 91; © Hulton-Deutsch
Collection / CORBIS: 104.

We would be happy to receive your comments
and suggestions, and give you any other
information concerning our material.
info@blackcat-cideb.com
blackcat-cideb.com

CISQ CISQ CERT
TEXTBOOKS AND
The quality of the publisher's
design, production and sales processes has
been certified to the standard of
UNI EN ISO 9001

ISBN 978-88-530-0640-0   Book + CD

Printed in Italy by Italgrafica, Novara

Contents

Chapters 1-8 are recorded on the accompanying CD.
Chapter 9 is downloadable from our website: www.cideb.it or www.blackcat-cideb.com.
These symbols indicate the beginning and end of the passages linked to the listening activities.

 www.blackcat-cideb.com passage downloadable from our site.

Robert Louis Stevenson (1892) by Girolamo Pieri Nerli.

Robert Louis Stevenson

Robert Louis Stevenson (1850-94) was born in Edinburgh. He studied law at Edinburgh University. He suffered from lung problems all his life but despite this was a great traveller and adventurer. He toured France and Belgium in a canoe and wrote about his adventures there in *An Inland Voyage* (1878). The following year he went to California, where he married Mrs Fanny Osborne. His novels include *Treasure Island* (1883), *The Strange Case of Dr Jekyll and Mr Hyde* (1886), *Kidnapped* (1886), *The Black Arrow* (1888), and *The Master of Ballantrae* (1889). In 1888, Stevenson left Britain because he hoped that a warmer climate would improve his health. He never returned. After sailing around the Pacific islands, he settled in Samoa. He became very interested in Polynesian culture and angry about European imperialism in the islands. During his last years in Samoa his health improved, and he wrote a lot. His best work from this period are two novellas – *The Beach at Falesà* (1893) and *The Ebb-Tide* (1894) – set in the South Seas; both expressed his passionate opposition to European imperialists who destroy beauty for profit.

Stevenson originally wrote *Treasure Island* to entertain his wife's son Lloyd. It was published in parts in a boys' magazine from October 1881 to January 1882 then appeared in book form in 1883. Although Stevenson himself did not consider the book among his best or most serious novels, it has always been and still is the most popular. It has been made into films, musicals, and television series. There is even a Treasure Island pirate game based on the characters in the novel.

Some people believe that the song that the pirates sing in the novel is based on a true story:

> *Fifteen men on the Dead Man's Chest*
> *Yo ho ho, and a bottle of rum!*

Edward Teach (*c.* 1680-1718), a pirate captain who was also known as Blackbeard (see page 58), abandoned a group of sailors on Dead Man's Chest Island in Deadman's Bay on Peter Island near Tortola in the Caribbean. He gave each man a bottle of rum. The island had no fresh water, and the Caribbean sun was very hot. A month later Teach returned to find that fifteen men had survived. The story and the song still fascinate audiences today: *Dead Man's Chest* is the name of the second *Pirates of the Caribbean* film with Johnny Depp.

1 Comprehension check
Answer the questions.

1 Where was Stevenson born?
2 Why did he leave Britain in 1888?
3 Where did he go to live?
4 Why did Stevenson write *Treasure Island*?

The Characters

Ben Gunn

Doctor Livesey

Billy Bones

Squire Trelawney

Jim

Long John Silver

ACTIVITIES

PET ① Book reviews

The people below are looking for a book to buy.

Below there are some reviews of different books by Robert Louis Stevenson. Decide which book (letters A-E) would be the most suitable for each person (numbers 1-3).

1 ☐ Patrick has a very boring job in an office, and every holiday he travels to some exciting, distant country. But he does not just go swimming in blue seas and walking about tourist places. He wants to know about the real life of the people that he meets and their problems. He always takes excellent and serious photos of the people that he meets.

2 ☐ Sylvia lives in New York City, and she loves crime and mystery stories. She likes knowing about the bad things that people do for money, for power and even for love. But she prefers mysteries with friendly detectives who always catch the criminal: she doesn't want to be too scared.

3 ☐ Sheila lives in small old town in northern Scotland, and she loves to imagine the past of this town. She especially likes reading about the old families — their loves and hates and battles. In other words, she wants to learn about history but in an entertaining way.

A **Dr Jekyll and Mr Hyde**

The models for this philosophical story were the popular, inexpensive thrillers of the period. It tells us about crime and horror in the streets of nighttime London. But Stevenson does more: he also gives us an exciting look at the good and evil in all of us.

B **Travels with a Donkey in the Cévennes**

This is one of the first books that presents hiking as a recreational sport. The author describes a 12-day hike through the Cévennes mountains in France with a donkey named Modestine — an important character in the book. The young Stevenson also gives many pleasant and accurate descriptions of the people.

C **In the South Seas**

This book was not at all successful when it came out. Stevenson fans expected his usual poetic style and imagination. This book,

7

though, has more in common with good modern investigative journalism. He shows us how the Europeans changed the lives of the peoples living in the islands of the South Pacific.

D The New Arabian Nights

This collection of short stories presents mysteries of the dark and criminal side of London. These mysteries are solved by the intelligent and elegant Prince Florizel. These stories show us the playful and fun-loving side of this great Scottish writer.

E The Master of Ballantrae

This novel tells the story of the conflict between two Scottish brothers: one good and the other evil. It takes place in 1745, an important moment in Scottish history. The story is entertaining and contains a lot about history. But today many people like this book because of the interesting literary techniques used by Stevenson.

Before you read

1 Vocabulary

Match each word (1-9) to the correct picture (A-I). Use a dictionary if you need help.

1 pigtail   2 cliffs   3 sword   4 scar   5 bacon

6 coins   7 chest   8 chest   9 shoulder

A ☐   B ☐   C ☐

  2 Listening

PET

You will hear about a boy called Jim Hawkins and a strange man who came to his family's inn, the Admiral Benbow. For each question, fill in the missing information in the numbered space.

The Sea Captain

His appearance
His hair was (**1**) ....
His coat was (**2**) ....

His meals
He drinks (**3**) ....
He eats (**4**) ....

His payment
He paid Jim's father with some (**5**) ....

His habits
During the day he looked for (**6**) ....
In the evening, he drank but he didn't (**7**) ....
very much.

The Captain

My name's Jim Hawkins, and my story begins in the year 1761, when I was eleven years old. My father and mother had an inn [1] called The Admiral Benbow by the sea near Bristol. [2] One day an old sea captain came into our inn. His skin was dark brown from the sun, and there was a scar on his face. His long hair was tied back in a pigtail. He wore a dirty blue coat, and under it he carried a sword.

'Give me some rum,' he said.

My father poured him a glass of rum and watched as he drank it slowly.

'This is a nice little place,' said the captain. 'Do you get much business?'

'Unfortunately, no,' my father replied.

'Good,' said the captain. 'I'll stay here a while. I'm a simple

1. **inn** : a small hotel which is also a pub.
2. **Bristol** : a city in the south-west of England. In the eighteenth century Bristol was a busy port and a centre of trade and shipping.

man. I eat eggs and bacon, and I drink rum.' He put some gold coins on the bar. 'Tell me when I've spent all that, and I'll give you some more,' he said.

He was very quiet. All day he walked on the cliffs by the sea, listening to the waves crashing[1] on the rocks below and looking out for ships through his telescope. All evening he sat in the bar beside the fire and drank rum. People tried to talk to him, but he usually didn't reply. Soon we learned to leave him in peace. Sometimes he sang quietly to himself an old sailor's song that started like this:

Fifteen men on the Dead Man's Chest,
Yo-ho-ho, and a bottle of rum!

I couldn't understand the words of the song. Did 'chest' mean a sea-chest like the captain's — a big box for carrying his clothes and other things — or did it mean the top part of the dead man's body, around his heart?

Every evening, when he came back from his walk, the captain asked if any sailor had come into the inn during the day. At first we thought he wanted company of people like himself, but then we realised that he didn't want to see other sailors. Whenever one came into the bar, he was even more silent than usual.

One day he gave me a silver coin. 'I want you to watch out for a sailor with one leg,' he said. 'I'll give you another silver coin on the first day of every month if you watch out for a man like that.'

Some nights, I dreamed that the sailor with one leg was running after me. They were terrifying dreams.

---

1. **crashing** : making a loud noise as they hit.

The Captain

When winter came, my father fell ill. My mother and I were very busy doing all the work of the inn and taking care of my poor father, so we didn't have time to pay much attention to the captain.

The captain was out as usual on the cliffs one cold morning when a sailor came into the Admiral Benbow. He was a strange pale [1] man with two fingers missing from one hand. 'Is my friend Billy Bones here?' he asked.

'I don't know your friend Billy Bones,' I replied.

'He's an old sea captain with a scar on his face.'

'Yes, he's staying here. He's out now, but he'll be back soon.'

'I'll wait for him.'

When the captain came in, he seemed shocked and angry to see his visitor. 'Black Dog!' he cried.

'Yes, it's me, your old friend Black Dog.'

'Well?' cried the captain. 'You've found me. Now — what do you want?'

'I want to drink a glass of rum with you, Bill, and talk.'

The captain sent me to get the rum then told me to leave them in peace. I went into the next room and listened, but at first they spoke quietly, so I couldn't hear what they were saying. After a while, though, they started to shout at each other. The captain cried 'No! Never!' then I heard the sounds of chairs and tables falling to the floor. I ran into the bar and saw that the captain and Black Dog were fighting with swords. Suddenly, Black Dog let out a cry of pain. The captain had cut him on the shoulder. Black Dog ran through the door and down the road.

---

1. **pale** : without much colour in his face.

'Get me some more rum, Jim,' said the captain.

His face was very pale, and he looked ill. When I came back with the rum, I found him lying [1] on the floor. Just then, the doctor came to see my father. We carried the captain up to his room. The doctor said, 'He drinks too much rum. It will kill him in the end.'

The next day, when I took some food to his room, the captain said to me, 'I must get away from here, Jim. Black Dog and the others want to kill me — especially the sailor with the wooden leg. They want my sea-chest. They're bad men, and they want to steal my treasure map. It's mine! Old Flint gave it to me before

1. **lying** : in a horizontal position.

he died! I was the first mate [1] on Captain Flint's ship, and Black Dog and the others were the crew. [2] They want that treasure, and they'll kill me to get the map! But first they'll give me the Black Spot. They always give you the Black Spot before they kill you. Help me, Jim. Watch out for them, and tell me if you see them, and I'll give you half the treasure!'

That night my poor father died. In the days that followed, my mother and I were very sad. At the same time we were very busy organising the funeral and doing all the work at the inn. The captain came downstairs during the day. We gave him his meals

1. **first mate** : the second in command of a ship, after the captain.
2. **crew** : the people who operate the ship.

as usual, but he didn't eat much. He drank rum and sang his ugly old song, even on the night before my father's funeral. He didn't speak to me, and I think he had forgotten the things he had told me when he was ill.

On the day after the funeral, a blind man came to the inn. 'Take me to the captain,' he said.

'I can't,' I replied.

The blind man held my arm so tightly that I cried out in pain. 'Take me to him now!' he cried in a cold cruel voice. I took him into the bar where the captain was drinking rum.

'Hello, Bill,' he said. 'I have something for you. Hold out your hand.'

The poor captain looked very pale and held out his hand. The blind man put something in it — a strange piece of paper cut into a circle — then he turned and left us quickly.

The captain looked at the circular piece of paper in his hand. On one side, it was completely black. On the other side the words, 'Tonight at ten o'clock' were written in small letters. I knew that this must be the Black Spot the captain had mentioned.

'Ten o'clock!' he cried. 'That's six hours from now! I can escape before they come to kill me!' But, as he spoke, his face went even paler, and he fell over, dead, at my feet.

I had never liked the man, but, when I saw that he was dead, I burst into tears.[1] It was the second death I had known, and I was still very sad about the first one.

---

1. **burst into tears** : suddenly began to cry.

Go back to the text

For each question, choose the correct answer — A, B, C or D.

1   The captain chose to stay at the Admiral Benbow because
  A ☐ it didn't cost much to eat and sleep there.
  B ☐ few people came there and the food was good.
  C ☐ he could watch the sea from the cliffs and few people came there.
  D ☐ he could watch the sea from the cliffs and he liked Jim.

2   Every day the captain asked if a sailor had come to the inn because
  A ☐ he wanted the company of another sailor like himself.
  B ☐ he was waiting for important news.
  C ☐ he knew that his enemies were looking for him.
  D ☐ a sailor was bringing him his sea-chest.

3   Black Dog came to see Billy Bones because
  A ☐ he wanted to take Billy Bones's money.
  B ☐ he wanted the treasure map.
  C ☐ he wanted Billy Bones to help him find the treasure.
  D ☐ he wanted Billy Bones to protect him from the blind pirate.

4   A good translation of the 'Black Spot' is
  A ☐ 'We are going to kill you if you don't help us.'
  B ☐ 'We are going to kill you if you don't pay us.'
  C ☐ 'We are going to kill you at this time.'
  D ☐ 'Run away or we will kill you.'

5   Jim took the blind man to Billy Bones because
  A ☐ the blind man hurt him badly.
  B ☐ Jim didn't like Billy Bones.
  C ☐ the blind man gave him some gold coins.
  D ☐ Jim thought that the blind man was Billy Bones' friend.

6   Billy Bones died because
  A ☐ he was so afraid of dying.
  B ☐ he was hurt by Black Dog.
  C ☐ he drank too much at the funeral of Jim's father.
  D ☐ he ran away from the Admiral Benbow.

7 Jim cried when Billy Bones died because

A ☐ he had become good friends with him.
B ☐ he felt sorry for him.
C ☐ he still felt very bad about his father's death.
D ☐ he was afraid.

2 Vocabulary

Fill in the word maps with the words in the box. The words must be related to the central word. There are seven words you do not need to use. All the words come from this chapter.

pain	ill	drink	face	tonight	month	leg	fingers
captain	sailor	shoulder	pour	bottle	glass	mate	
dead	death	tears	died	cry	rum	cut	scar	day
morning	evening	skin	hour	hand	sword	year	kill

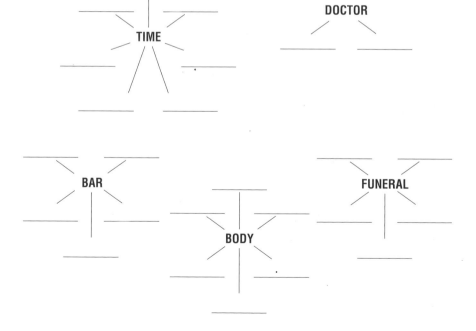

Before you read

  Listening

PET

Listen to the first part of Chapter Two. Choose the correct picture and put a tick (✓) in the box.

1 Where does Jim want to go with his mother?

A ☐   B ☐   C ☐

2 What time is it?

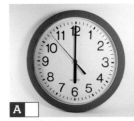 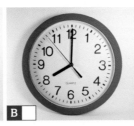 

A ☐   B ☐   C ☐

3 What does Jim's mother want to take from the sea-chest?

A ☐   B ☐   C ☐

4 What was the man in front holding?

A ☐   B ☐   C ☐

CHAPTER **TWO**

The Treasure Map

I ran to my mother and told her that the captain was dead. Then
I told her all about Black Dog and the blind man, and I told her
what the captain had said to me when he was ill. 'Mother,' I said,
'I think we are in danger. They'll come here to kill him at ten
o'clock tonight. They are terrible, violent men, and they want
the treasure map from the captain's sea-chest. I'm afraid that
they'll kill us if we are here when they come. Let's go to the
village and ask some of the men to come back here and help us.'

'No,' said my mother. 'Those village men are big and strong,
but they are not very brave. They're all afraid of pirates.'

'Then we must run away, Mother,' I said. 'We must go before
ten o'clock!'

'Don't worry,' she replied. 'It's only six o'clock now. We have
plenty of time. The captain owed [1] us money. Get the key to his
sea-chest, Jim. We'll open it and take the money he owes us.'

---

1. **owed** : needed to give us money.

Though it filled me with horror to search a dead man's body, I did so. I found the key on a piece of string around his neck. We ran up to the captain's room and opened the sea-chest. At the bottom of the chest we found a bag of gold and a packet of papers. My mother said, 'I'll show these pirates that I'm an honest woman. I'll take just what the captain owed us and no more.' It took a long time to count out what he owed us, because the gold coins were from all over the world, and my mother only knew the value of the English coins. As she was counting, we heard a sound in the distance. I looked out of the window and saw a light on the road coming towards the Admiral Benbow.

'Let's go, Mother!' I cried. 'The pirates are coming!'

'All right,' she said. 'But I haven't got all my money yet.'

I took the packet of papers. 'Let's take this instead!' I said, and we ran out of the house.

'You keep running, my boy!' cried my mother. 'I can't. I feel ill!' With those words, she fainted, [1] and I pulled her behind a tree. A moment later, seven pirates came to the door of the inn. From my hiding place [2] behind the tree, I could see that the man in front was holding a lantern — the light I had seen from the captain's bedroom window. After him came three men holding hands. The one in the middle was the blind man. 'Go in and find Bill!' he cried.

'Yes, sir!' replied the others, and they ran in. After a minute, one of the men came out and said, 'Bill's dead, and there's no one else in the house.'

---

1. **fainted** : lost consciousness.
2. **hiding place** : secret place where he cannot be seen.

'Then get the chest, you idiot!' cried the blind man.

I heard them running up the stairs. Another minute passed, then the window of the captain's room opened, and a man inside called down to the blind man, 'Pew! Someone's been here before us! The chest is open!'

'Is it there?' asked Pew.

'The money's there,' replied the man at the window.

'Not the money, you idiot, the treasure map! Is it there?'

'No, sir.'

'It's that boy!' said Pew. 'He must be hiding somewhere. Find him!'

I could hear the pirates while they kicked open doors and broke furniture in the Admiral Benbow, then they ran out of the house and started searching the land around it. Suddenly one of them cried, 'Look! Someone's coming! Four men on horses! They must be the customs officers. Come on, Pew! We've got the money, so forget the map and let's go!'

The pirates ran away, leaving Pew alone. Trying to run away with no one to help him, the blind man ran into the road. The road was dark and the four horses were coming very quickly, so that the men did not see Pew. He fell over and one of the horses kicked him in the head and killed him. I came out from my hiding place and saw that the four men were customs officers.

They went away on their horses, hoping to catch the pirates as they tried to get back to their ship, but they were too late: when they reached [1] the shore, [2] they saw the pirate ship sailing out to sea in the moonlight.

---

1. **reached** : arrived at.
2. **shore** : the land next to the sea.

They returned and listened to my story. We carried my mother to the village and then went back to the Admiral Benbow. Everything in the house was broken. It was a terrible mess. [1]

'What were they looking for, Hawkins? Money?' asked one of the customs officers.

'No, sir,' I said. 'They found the money. They were looking for this.' I showed him the captain's packet of papers.

'I'll take that now, boy,' he said.

'I would prefer Doctor Livesey...'

'That's right,' he said, 'a gentleman and a magistrate.'

We found Dr Livesey at the Hall with Squire Trelawney. I looked at the squire with interest: I'd never seen him close up before. He was a big man with a red face and bright eyes. As I told the story, they both listened in amazement. [2] A servant brought me food and drink. I ate quickly and listened as the doctor and the squire talked about our adventure.

'Have you heard of Captain Flint?' asked the doctor.

'Heard of him?' cried the squire. 'He was the most famous pirate on the seas! Everyone was afraid of him! He attacked so many Spanish ships that I felt almost proud that he was an Englishman!'

'And was he rich?'

'Oh, yes! He had all the gold from those Spanish ships!'

Dr Livesey put the captain's packet on the table. 'Shall we open it, Jim?' he asked.

'Yes!' I replied, and the squire and I watched as the doctor opened the packet very carefully. Inside was a map of an island. The longitude and latitude were written at the top of the map.

1. **mess** : state of untidiness, disorder.
2. **amazement** : great surprise.

The island was about nine miles [1] long and five miles wide. It had two big harbours — one in the north and one in the south — and in the middle was a hill called 'the Spyglass'. [2] By a river in the forest just south of the Spyglass, was a large wooden building called the fort. There was a small island marked Skeleton Island in the southern harbour. Three red crosses indicated different places, two in the north of the island and one in the south-west. By the cross in the north-west, Captain Flint had written, 'The guns are here'. By the cross in the north-east, he had written, 'The bars of silver are here'. By the cross in the south-west, he had written, 'Most of the treasure is here'.

On the back of the map were instructions about how to find the treasure:

> *Go to the tallest tree in the area. From that point you can see the top of Spyglass Hill and you can also see Skeleton Island. The treasure is buried [3] by that tree.*
>
> *John Flint*

'Livesey!' cried the squire. 'I'll go to Bristol tomorrow and buy us a ship and a crew. Young Hawkins here will be the cabin boy, [4] you'll be the ship's doctor, and I'll be the captain! Soon, we'll be ready to sail to the island and find the treasure!'

---

1. **miles** : a mile is about 1.6 kilometres.
2. **Spyglass** : 'spyglass' is an eighteenth-century word for 'telescope'. This suggests that from that hill a person can see the whole island and the surrounding sea.
3. **buried** : under the ground.
4. **cabin boy** : the youngest member of the crew, who acts as servant to the captain and other officers.

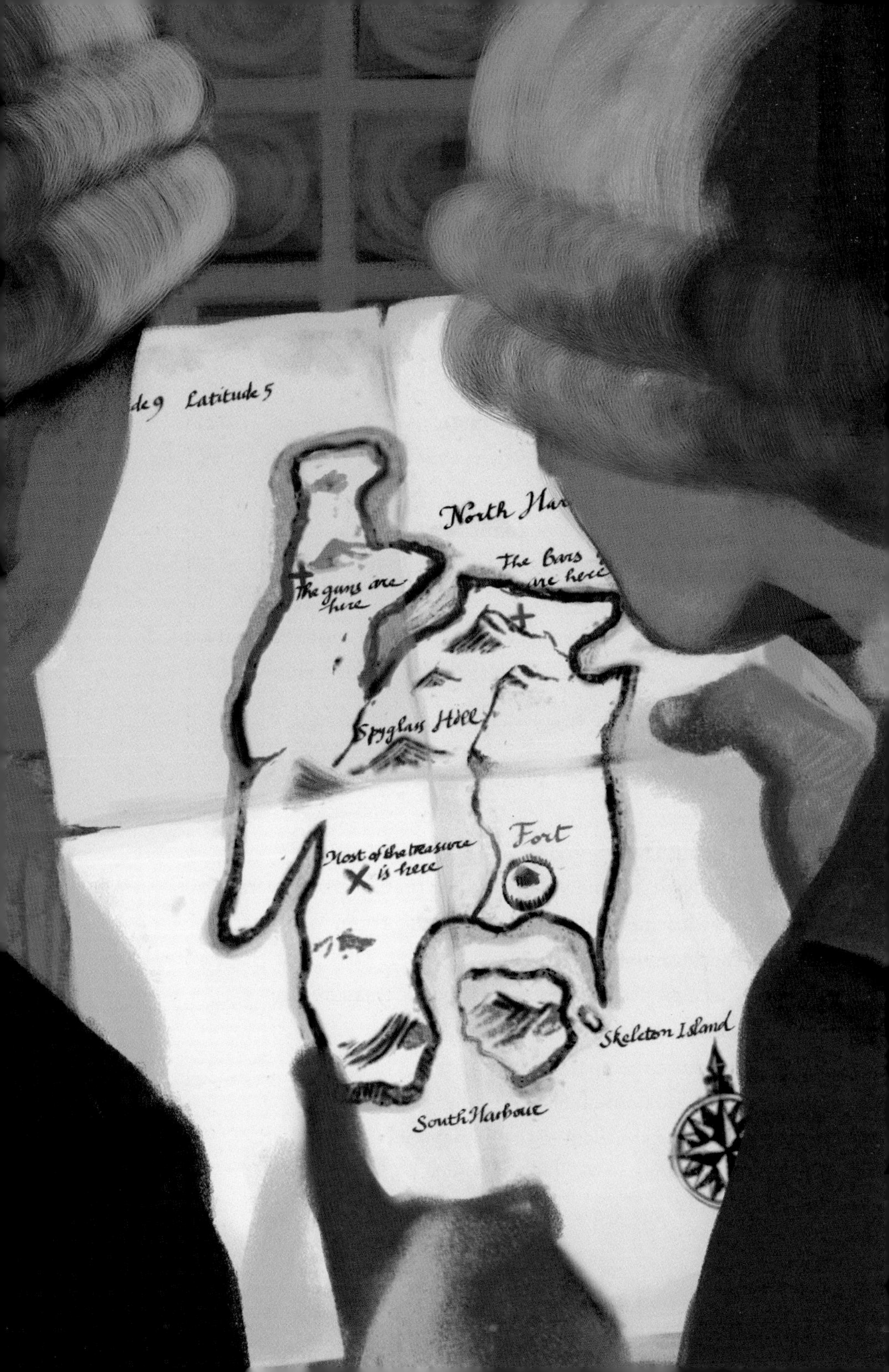
Latitude 5
The bars
are here
The guns are here
Spyglass Hill
Fort
Most of the treasure is here
Skeleton Island
South Harbour

Go back to the text

1 Comprehension check

Match the phrases in columns A and B to make complete sentences. There are three phrases in column B that you do not need to use.

A

1 ☐ Jim wanted to go to the village

2 ☐ Jim's mother didn't want to go to the village

3 ☐ Jim's mother wanted to open the captain's sea-chest

4 ☐ Jim and his mother were still at the Admiral Benbow when the pirates arrived

5 ☐ The pirates came to the Admiral Benbow

6 ☐ The customs officers came quickly to the Admiral Benbow

7 ☐ The customs officers could not catch the pirates

8 ☐ Squire Trelawney was proud of the pirate Captain Flint

9 ☐ The squire was going to Bristol to buy a ship

B

A because they were already on their ship.

B because it took her a long time to count the coins.

C because he wanted to go to Treasure Island.

D because she knew that the men there were not very brave.

E because he wanted to ask the village men to protect them.

F because they saw the pirate ship.

G because she wanted to look for the treasure map.

H because he was very hungry.

I because the Spanish were afraid of him.

J because Captain Flint was very rich.

K because she wanted the money that he owed her.

L because they wanted to kill Bill.

'I told her that the captain was dead.'

Look at how we change direct speech into reported speech.

- *'The inn **is** near Bristol,' he said.*
  → *He said that the inn **was** near Bristol.*
- *'I **eat** only eggs and bacon,' he said.*
  → *He said that **he ate** only eggs and bacon.*
- *'I **am** going to get the coins,' my mother said.*
  → *My mother said that **she was** going to get the coins.*
- *'I **will** give **you** part of **my** treasure,' the captain said.*
  → *The captain said that he **would** give **me** part of **his** treasure.*
- *'He **went** out to the cliffs,' I said.*
  → *I said that he **had gone** out to the cliffs.*
- *'The doctor **has arrived**,' she said.*
  → *She said that the doctor **had arrived**.*
- *'I **can** see the ship with **my** telescope,' he said.*
  *He said that he **could** see the ship with **his** telescope.*

We generally use 'told' with a direct object.

- *I **told him** that the blind man had arrived.*
- *They **told me** that the captain was dangerous.*

2 Reported speech

A   Change the direct speech into reported speech.

1   'I have something for you,' the blind man told the captain.
2   'I want to drink a glass of rum with you,' Black Dog told the captain.
3   'I can escape before they come to kill me!' said the captain.
4   'I will wait for him,' said Black Dog.
5   'Old Flint gave it to me,' the captain said.

B   Change the reported speech into direct speech.

1   He said that a strange sailor had come to his inn.
2   I told him that I would look for the sailor with one leg.

3   She said that she had just one son.

4   He said that he knew about the treasure map.

5   She told me that her son had helped the captain.

3 **Summary**

Number the paragraphs in the right order to make a summary of Chapters One-Two.

A ☐ The day after the funeral, a blind man came to see the captain and give him the 'Black Spot'. The captain became so frightened that he died.

B ☐ This captain spent his days on the cliffs looking for ships. He also gave Jim a silver coin to look out for a sailor with one leg.

C ☐ The captain told Jim that Black Dog and other pirates, especially one with a wooden leg, wanted to kill him to get a treasure map. That night Jim's father died.

D ☐ When Jim told his mother that the captain was dead, she wanted to open his sea-chest. The captain owed her money.

E ☐ Jim and one of the customs officers took the captain's papers to Dr Livesey and Squire Trelawney. When the squire saw the treasure map he decided to buy a ship and sail off in search of Treasure Island.

F ☐ In the winter Jim's father fell ill. Then a sailor named Black Dog came to see the captain. The two men fought with their swords, and Black Dog ran away.

G ☐ The pirates soon discovered that the map was gone. Just then four customs officers arrived on horses. Six of the pirates escaped, but blind Pew was killed by a horse.

H ☐ Before she could count out the coins, six pirates and blind Pew arrived. Jim and his mother ran out of the house and hid behind a tree.

I ☐ Jim Hawkins's parents had an inn by the sea near Bristol called the Admiral Benbow. One day an old sea captain with a scar came to stay with them.

Pirates: The Real Story

Treasure Island is a work of imagination. Its author Robert Louis Stevenson never met a pirate. However, he knew a lot about sailing and ships. His grandfather and father were both lighthouse engineers, and the young Stevenson travelled with them by ship around Scotland. His descriptions of ships at sea have convinced many experienced sailors.

But the heart of his book are the pirates and they, too, seem real because of their cruelty, their violence, their wild parties and their cleverness. Partly, this is because Stevenson, like all great writers,

Recruiting for a pirate ship in the 17th century (1932) by Arthur David McCormick. The pirates, sitting on the left, interview a possible new member of their company, standing on the right.

observed real men and then used them as the basis for his literary creations. But Stevenson also read about historical pirates in Captain Charles Johnson's popular book of 1724 *A General History of Robberies and Murders of the Most Notorious Pyrates*. It contains biographies of all the most famous pirates of the 'Golden Age of Piracy' (1650-1725). Squire Trelawney says that the imaginary Captain Flint sailed with the real and terrible Edward Teach, better known as Blackbeard (1675-1718). The squire is even proud that Blackbeard was an Englishman. With the mention of Blackbeard, Stevenson places his story in the real world of the pirates of the Caribbean.

Historical piracy in the Caribbean and Atlantic Ocean began soon after the discovery of the Americas by Europeans in 1492. In the beginning, Spain dominated the New World, and mined enormous amounts of silver in Mexico and Peru. Fleets of ships took silver and gold from Veracruz in Mexico to the port of Seville in Spain. Of course, these ships full of silver and gold were tempting targets [1] for the Dutch, French and English. In the early 1500s these nations did not have important navies of their own. So, their rulers gave permission to private captains to attack Spanish ships. These captains were known as privateers, and perhaps the two most famous of all were England's Sir Francis Drake (1540-1596) and Sir John Hawkins (1532-1595). These privateers worked for England's protestant Queen Elizabeth I. They helped to make their Protestant queen rich and to fight her war against Catholic Spain.

Privateers continued to be important in the wars between the major European powers until the early 1700s. For example, they played an important part in Queen Anne's War (1702-1713), one of the wars

---

1. **targets** : objects to attack.

Captain Morgan defeats a Spanish warship on Lake Maracaibo in 1669
(17th century) by an unknown English artist. Lake Maracaibo is in Venezuela.

fought between Britain and France. But after the war ended, thousands of sailors and privateers were without work. Many of these became pirates to survive.

Another reason sailors became pirates was the horrible life of common sailors during this period. The captains of warships and merchant ships were often tyrants [1] who used horrible physical punishment on their men. Also, the common sailors had terrible food and sometimes they were not even paid. The famous writer and lexicographer Dr Samuel Johnson (1709-1784) wrote that it was better for man to be in prison than a sailor on a ship: 'A man in prison has more room, better food, and commonly better company'. Or as the pirate Captain Bartholomew Roberts (1682-1722) explained: 'An

1. **tyrants** : people in authority who are severe and unjust.

honest sailor gets little food, low pay and hard work. A pirate gets lots of food, drink, fun, freedom and power. Who wouldn't choose to be pirate? The worst that can happen to you as pirate is that they hang you. My motto is this: A merry [1] life and a short life.'

Most pirates of this period were just common sailors. They were happy to live a short dangerous life of pleasure and freedom instead of the short, dangerous and sad life on a British warship or merchant ship.

Life on pirate ships was a kind of democracy. The captain of a pirate ship was elected by his men, and, if they were not satisfied with him, they could change him. The pirate captain, unlike a captain of the British navy, commanded only during the battles. Also, he had to lead his men into the battle and show exceptional courage. Pay was also much different on a pirate ship: everybody on the ship received almost the same pay. They also all received the same amount of good food and drink: a common sailor's food on a merchant ship or warship was often full of worms.

With regards to fun, pirates were famous for their wild parties. During every real pirate party the ship's guns were fired, and during one party the pirates under the command of the famous pirate and privateer Captain Henry Morgan (1635-1688) blew up their ship by mistake. Pirates were also famous for their love of music. Musicians played not only during their parties but also during battle.

But pirates were not just common sailors from Europe, they were also Africans. By the 1600s thousands of Africans were brought to the Caribbean as slaves. Many of them ran away and sometimes these slaves joined up with pirates. The important thing for a white pirate was not the colour of a man's skin, but his knowledge of the

---

1.   **merry** : happy and cheerful.

Pirates from the film **Pirates of the Caribbean: The Curse of the Black Pearl** (2003). Hollywood has always made films about pirates, and the most recent films star Johnny Depp (see page 93).

sea. Perhaps one third of pirate crews were Africans. Some Africans even became the captains of pirate ships.

But pirates also joined African tribes. In the early 1720s a group of pirates escaping from the British navy went to live with the Kru people of West Africa. The Kru were famous for their ability at sea in long canoes.

So, for about 70 years pirates were a real power in the Atlantic and Caribbean. They easily found sailors who wanted to join and ships to attack. Also, the Caribbean with its many islands and secret harbours made it easy for them to hide. But gradually things became more and more difficult for them. This was because Britain began to build a powerful navy, and they did everything they could to catch and kill the pirates. When a British warship captured a pirate ship, the pirates were often killed and then hung from the mast of a ship at the entrance of the port. Sometimes as many as 30 dead pirates could be seen hanging under a beautiful blue Caribbean sky: the British navy fought terror with terror.

In the end, the efficiency of the British navy ended the short rule of these common sailors and former slaves. However, the legends of these colourful characters who lived outside the law continue to fascinate us.

1 Comprehension check
Answer the questions.

1 Why are Stevenson's descriptions of sailing so accurate?
2 How did Stevenson construct his descriptions of pirates?
3 What was the origin of piracy in the Caribbean?
4 Why did common sailors become pirates?
5 Why was a pirate ship democratic?
6 Why did Africans become pirates?
7 Who were the Kru?
8 How long were pirates an important force in the Caribbean?
9 What advantages did the geography of the Caribbean offer pirates?
10 Why did pirates begin to lose their power in the Caribbean?
11 How did the British frighten pirates?

2 Discussion
With your partner discuss the following topics, and then report your ideas to the class.

• why pirates continue to fascinate people today
• things about pirates that you consider positive
• things about pirates that you consider negative

INTERNET PROJECT

Connect to the Internet and go to www.blackcat-cideb.com or www.cideb.it. Insert the title or part of the title of the book into our search engine. Open the page for *Treasure Island*. Click on the Internet project link.

With your partner find out more about one of the following pirate topics. Download some pictures too, and then present a short report to the class.

▶ Weapons – the ones used by individual pirates and the ship's cannons
▶ Calico Jack and Anne Bonny
▶ The Jolly Roger and other pirate flags
▶ Where Gallows Point and Execution Dock were and why they were famous

Before you read

 1 Listening

Listen to the beginning of Chapter Three. You will hear about the squire in Bristol. Decide if each sentence is correct or incorrect. If it is correct, put a tick (✓) in the box under A for YES. If it not correct, put a tick (✓) in the box under B for NO.

		A Yes	B No
1	*Hispaniola* is the name of an inn in Bristol.	☐	☐
2	The squire has not yet found a crew for the ship.	☐	☐
3	Long John Silver will be the captain of the ship.	☐	☐
4	Long John Silver does not have two legs.	☐	☐
5	The squire did not keep the treasure map a secret.	☐	☐

To Sea!

The next day, the squire left for Bristol. He took three of his most honest servants with him to be part of the crew of our ship. As they were leaving, Dr Livesey said to the squire, 'Don't tell anyone about the treasure map. The pirates who searched the Admiral Benbow want that map, and they know that Jim has it. All their friends on the ship probably know it now too. We must be very careful.'

Don't worry,' said the squire. 'I won't say a word.'

I stayed at Dr Livesey's house, because the doctor was afraid that the pirates would come back to find me and the treasure map. After three weeks, we received a letter from the squire:

> *My dear Livesey and Hawkins,*
>
> *Finally everything is ready for our sea adventure! Everyone here has helped me. As soon as I tell them why we need the ship, they do all they can to help us! I've bought a fine ship called the 'Hispaniola', and I've found an excellent crew. Fortunately, the*

day I bought the ship I met a man called Long John Silver. He's an old sailor, married to a woman he met on his travels. He knows all the sailors in Bristol. I like the man and feel sorry for him, because he has only one leg, so I've hired[1] him as the ship's cook. He has helped me to find other crew members.

Come to Bristol as quickly as you can, and we'll sail the next day!

Yours,

John Trelawney

Two things about this letter worried me: first, it was clear that the squire had told people about the treasure map; and, secondly, I was afraid that Long John Silver might be the same one-legged sailor the captain had mentioned. But I was so excited about going to sea that soon I stopped thinking about these things and thought only of the wonderful adventures ahead.

That last night before we went to Bristol, I stayed with my mother at the Admiral Benbow. The squire had bought new furniture for the inn and had hired a boy to help my mother while I was gone. It was only when I saw that boy that I fully realised that I was leaving my home, but I had no time to feel sad. The next morning, the doctor and I went to Bristol. We went straight to the port. I looked around in amazement. There were great ships from every nation and sailors with gold earrings and long pigtails. The air smelled of the salty sea. To me it was the smell of adventure!

The squire showed us round the *Hispaniola*. It was a fine ship, and the crew smiled and waved[2] at us as we came on board. The

---

1. **hired** : given him a job.   2. **waved** : moved their hands to say hello.

squire introduced me to Long John Silver. He was a big tall man with a crutch under one arm and a parrot on his shoulder. He had a big pale face, bright eyes and blond hair. The squire said to me, 'Jim, you stay here with Long John while I show the doctor my cabin.'

The squire and the doctor went off together, probably to drink a glass of wine in the squire's cabin to celebrate our first evening on board. I stood on the deck[1] with Long John, and he told me about all the ships we could see at the port. He was a friendly man, and soon I felt sure that he wasn't the one-legged sailor of the captain's stories and my bad dreams. I knew what kind of men pirates were: they were cruel and violent, not at all like this kind, friendly, smiling man.

As Long John was talking, I suddenly saw Black Dog in the crowd below us in the port. He saw me and ran away.

'Look!' I cried, interrupting Long John. 'That's Black Dog! He's a pirate!'

Long John Silver looked in the direction I was pointing, with a look of great surprise on his face. 'A pirate? Is he really? What did you say his name was?'

'Black Dog!'

'Ah, yes! I've often seen him with another man — a blind man,' said Long John.

'That's Pew!' I cried.

'I think you're right. Yes, I think his name's Pew,' said Long John in amazement. 'Well, you're a clever boy. I think we'll be great friends, you and I.'

---

1. **deck** : top floor of the ship.

That evening, I helped Long John prepare dinner. While he was cooking, Long John put his parrot in a cage in the ship's kitchen.

'I call my parrot Captain Flint, like the famous pirate,' said Long John, smiling.

The parrot suddenly squawked [1] and cried, 'Pieces of eight! Pieces of eight!' [1]

After dinner, Long John and the rest of the crew sat on the deck. Long John started singing a song I knew well, and then the crew sang along with him:

Fifteen men on the Dead Man's Chest,
Yo-ho-ho, and a bottle of rum!

Early the next morning, the *Hispaniola* left the port and sailed out into the open sea. Our voyage was very pleasant. The *Hispaniola* sailed on through sunny days and starry nights. One evening, after we had been at sea for three weeks, Mr Trelawney told us that we were close to the island. I stood on the deck with the rest of the crew, looking at the horizon, hoping to see land. Then I went down to the kitchen to get an apple. There was a big barrel in the kitchen, nearly as tall as I was. It had been full of apples at the start of the voyage, but now there were only a few left. I climbed into the barrel to get an apple, then I sat down in the barrel to eat it. After a few minutes, I heard two people come into the kitchen. They were talking, and I recognised one was Long John Silver. I was going to stand up and show myself, but when I heard what Long John Silver was saying, I stayed where I was and was very quiet.

---

1. **squawked** : made a loud noise, as parrots do.
2. **pieces of eight** : silver coins, also known as the Spanish dollar.

'I was the cook on Old Flint's ship, said Long John. 'We had some great adventures in those days.'

'I hear Captain Flint was the best!' said the other man, and I recognised his voice. He was a young sailor in the crew called Dick.

'Yes,' said Long John. 'Flint was the best pirate captain, but he wasn't the strongest man on that ship. He was afraid of me. I had more control of the crew than he had. Most of them are here, now, on this ship, ready for a new adventure. The life of the pirate is the best life, Dick! It's dangerous, and you might finish up dead like Pew, but, if not, you can end your days as rich as a gentleman, with lots of good stories to tell your grandchildren. So, what do you say? Are you with us or against us?'

'I'm with you, John!' said Dick. 'When do you plan to take over [1] the ship?'

'Not yet,' said Long John. 'Livesey and Trelawney have the map. We'll let them lead us to the treasure, and then we'll kill them!'

Inside the apple barrel, I held my breath. [2] I realised that the lives of all honest men on the ship now depended on me alone.

Just then a voice from the deck cried, 'Land Ho!' [3]

1. **take over** : take control of.
2. **held my breath** : did not breathe (because he was afraid of making a sound).
3. **Land Ho!** : what sailors shout when they see land.

Go back to the text

1 Comprehension check
Answer the following questions.

1   What was going to be Long John Silver's job on the ship?

2   How did Long John help the squire?

3   What disturbed Jim about the squire's letter?

4   Why did Jim decide that Long John is not a pirate?

5   What did Captain Flint say?

6   How did Jim discover Long John's real plans?

7   What were these plans?

8   Why, according to Long John, was it great to be a pirate?

PET **2** Sentence transformation
For each question, complete the second sentence so that it means the same as the first, using no more than three words.

0   Though it filled me with horror to search a dead man's body, I did so.
It filled me with horror to search a dead man's body ...but.................
I did it anyway.

1   He must be hiding somewhere.
I .... that he is hiding somewhere.

2   I was so excited about going to sea that soon I stopped thinking about these things.
I stopped thinking about these things ....
I was so excited about going to sea.

3   I had no time to feel sad.
I did not .... to feel sad.

4   I knew what kind of men pirates were.
I knew .... like.

5   Captain Flint was the best!
Nobody .... Captain Flint!

6   When do you plan to take over the ship?
When are you .... take over the ship?

45

❸ Crossword

Use the clues below and do the crossword puzzle. All the words come from Chapters Two-Three.

Across

3   The opposite of 'kind'.
4   Tables, chairs and beds
7   A bird that can say human words.
8   Give somebody a job.
12 The opposite of 'in front of'.
13 A big cylinder used as a container.
15 The opposite of 'enemies'.
16 Looking for.

Down

1   The ability to control fear when facing danger.
2   The imaginary lines used to measure distances from north to south.
5   Circular jewellery on the ears.
6   A lot of gold, gems and other valuable things.
9   Area of water protected from the open sea.
10 If you can't see, you are ....
11 Truthful and sincere.
14 He lost consciousness = He ....

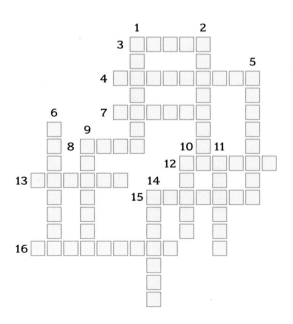

Before you read

1 Listening

Fill in the gaps with the words in the box. Then listen to the beginning of Chapter Four to check your answers.

gave	whole	ran	got	stood	hungry	called
became	stopped	was	got	took	fresh	came

Long John and Dick (**1**) .... out onto the deck to see the island. When they were gone, I (**2**) .... out of the barrel and ran out too. By the time I (**3**) .... there, the (**4**) .... crew was on deck, looking out to sea, but it (**5**) .... too dark to see anything. Then suddenly the moon (**6**) .... out from behind a cloud, and we saw land on the horizon. Mr Trelawney (**7**) .... up and spoke to the crew. 'Has anyone here ever been on that island before?' he asked.

'I have, sir,' said Long John. 'A ship I was on (**8**) .... there once to get (**9**) .... water.'

'And where did your ship land?'

'In the southern harbour, sir, behind the small island. Once pirates used this island, and they (**10**) .... it Skeleton Island.

'Yes, that's what it says here,' said Mr Trelawney, looking at the map in his hand. 'Have a look at this, Long John, and show me the best place to land.'

Long John (**11**) .... the map with a (**12**) .... look on his face, but soon that (**13**) .... a look of discontent: the map the squire (**14**) .... him was not the captain's treasure map; it was a copy, showing the island and naming its parts, but without the three red crosses.

The Island

Long John and Dick ran out onto the deck to see the island. When they were gone, I got out of the barrel and ran out too. By the time I got there, the whole crew was on deck, looking out to sea, but it was too dark to see anything. Then suddenly the moon came out from behind a cloud, and we saw land on the horizon. Mr Trelawney stood up and spoke to the crew. 'Has anyone here ever been on that island before?' he asked.

'I have, sir,' said Long John. 'A ship I was on stopped there once to get fresh water.'

'And where did your ship land?' [1]

'In the southern harbour, sir, behind a small island. Once pirates used that island, and they called it Skeleton Island.

'Yes, that's what it says here,' said Mr Trelawney, looking at the map in his hand. 'Have a look at this, Long John, and show me the best place to land.'

Long John took the map with a hungry look on his face, but

---

1. **land** : arrive at a place from the sea.

soon that became a look of discontent: the map the squire gave him was not the captain's treasure map; it was a copy, showing the island and naming its parts, but without the three red crosses.

Long John showed the squire the best place to land, then he came to me and put his hand on my shoulder. 'It's a great island for a boy to explore,' he said. 'You can swim and climb trees and hunt [1] goats. If you want to explore the island, just tell me. I'll make a picnic and we can go!' He smiled at me and went back to the kitchen. My heart was beating very fast all the time he was speaking to me. While I listened to his kind words, I thought about the cruel words I had heard him say to Dick as I sat in the apple barrel. Long John Silver now filled me with horror; I was terrified by his brutality, his dishonesty, and his power.

Mr Trelawney spoke to the crew again: 'Tomorrow morning we will land on the island. I want to thank you all for your good work. Tonight at dinner there will be a glass of rum for every man on board!' After this, he and the doctor went down to the captain's cabin to eat their dinner. I went down with them. As soon as we were alone, I told them what I had heard as I sat in the apple barrel. The squire and the doctor looked at me in amazement. The doctor poured me a glass of wine and said, 'Thank you, Jim. You're a clever, brave boy.'

'What shall we do?' asked the squire.

'Well,' said the doctor. 'We know that the mutineers [2] don't plan to attack us until we've found the treasure. That gives us some time. Do you think all the men are against us?'

'No!' said the squire. 'Three of them are my servants —

---

1. **hunt** : look for and shoot.
2. **mutineers** : sailors who take over the ship.

Redruth, Hunter, and Joyce. I have known them for years, and I'm sure they're honest.'

'So there are six of us, including Jim here, and there are nineteen of them. But perhaps among the nineteen there are other honest men who wouldn't hurt us. Jim, you must listen to their conversations and find out if any other men want to help us.'

The next morning, we reached the island. The squire gave guns to the men he was sure of and half the crew got off the ship to explore it. I decided to go with them. I jumped quickly into a boat and kept my head down but Long John looked over from the other boat and asked, 'Is that you, Jim?'

As soon as the boat arrived on land I jumped out of the boat and ran into some trees to hide.

The island was a strange, sad place, covered with grey forest. In the middle, there was the hill called the Spyglass high above the forest. After some time I heard voices and I moved quietly nearer, so that I could hear what they were saying. I looked out from behind a tree and saw Long John talking to another man — a member of the crew called Tom. They couldn't see me.

'So, are you with us or against us, Tom?' asked Long John.

'I'm against you, John!' replied the other. 'You know that I'm an honest man. I'll do my duty [1] and serve the captain!'

Just then a terrible scream came out of the forest.

'What was that?' asked Tom.

Long John smiled and said, 'Oh, that's probably Allan.'

'Allan? What? Have you killed poor Allan just because he was an honest sailor? We were friends once, Long John, but I'm not

---

1. **my duty** : my job, what I should do.

your friend any more. You'll have to kill me too if you want to stop me doing my duty!'

With that, the brave sailor walked away. Long John took his knife and threw it at Tom's back. The knife hit Tom just between the shoulders, and he fell to the ground dead.

In my hiding place, I felt faint with fear. [1] They had already killed two honest men; if they found me, they would kill me too! I ran into the forest, trying to get as far away from the mutineers as possible. But, as I ran, I saw, ahead of me, a strange creature running between the trees. It seemed half-man, half-beast, and I was afraid. With the mutineers behind me and this man-beast in front of me, there was nowhere I could go. I stopped and took out my gun. The man-beast came out from behind a tree, and fell to his knees in front of me. I could see now that he was a white man. His skin was dark brown from the sun, but his eyes were pale blue. His clothes were dirty rags [2] and goatskins.

'Who are you?' I asked.

'I'm Ben Gunn,' he replied, 'and I haven't spoken to another man for the last three years! It's terrible to be alone so long! I was one of the crew of Captain Flint's ship,' he said. 'Have you heard of Captain Flint?'

'Yes, I have!' I replied. The man looked wild and a little mad, but that was not surprising, if, as he said, he had been alone on the island for three years. I decided to trust [3] him. I told him my name and then I told him the whole story of the treasure map and Long John Silver. He listened, then he said to me. 'I'll help you if you help me. Your captain must give me a thousand

---

1. **faint with fear** : weak because I was so afraid.
2. **rags** : very old torn clothes.
3. **trust** : believe in his honesty.

pounds and take me back to England. If he agrees to do that, I'll tell you all I know and help you all I can.'

'I'm sure that he'll agree,' I said.

'I was on the ship when old Flint went to the island to hide his treasure,' said Ben Gunn. 'He went with six sailors, but he came back alone. He had killed them all! He didn't want anyone alive to know where he'd hidden that treasure. Three years ago, I was on another ship. As we were sailing past this island, I said, "Flint's treasure is hidden there! Let's go and find it!" We stopped and searched the island for twelve days, but we never found the treasure. In the end, the others got angry with me. They got back on the ship and sailed away, leaving me here with nothing but a gun for hunting goats. And I've been here alone for three long years. For three years I've had nothing to eat except goat's meat.' He stopped suddenly, then, with a hungry look, he asked me, 'Do you have any cheese?'

'There's lots of cheese on our ship, but how can I get back there? I'm afraid to go in the boats with the pirates. They might kill me.'

'Ah!' said Ben Gunn. 'I have a boat. I made it with my own hands. It's on the east side of the island, hidden behind a big white rock. We can go to the ship in my little boat when it gets dark.'

Just then we heard the sound of guns. Ben Gunn and I ran through the forest towards it. Then the guns stopped. We continued running, and finally we came to a large wooden building at the edge of the forest, on a cliff by the sea. I realised that this must be the fort. I was very surprised to see that the Union Jack [1] was waving [2] in the wind above it.

1. **Union Jack** :

2. **waving** : moving about.

Go back to the text

PET ❶ Comprehension check

Decide if each sentence is correct or incorrect. If it is correct, mark A. If it not correct, mark B.

	A	B
1 Long John showed Mr Trelawney where to land on the island.	☐	☐
2 Dr Livesey and Squire Trelawney were not surprised to learn that Long John was a pirate.	☐	☐
3 Most of the crew were mutineers.	☐	☐
4 Long John killed Allan.	☐	☐
5 Jim was afraid of Ben Gunn when he first saw him.	☐	☐
6 Captain Flint left Ben Gunn on the island.	☐	☐
7 Ben Gunn said that he would help Jim and his friends for some cheese.	☐	☐
8 The pirate flag was waving over the fort when Jim and Ben arrived there.	☐	☐

❷ Vocabulary

**Find the opposites to the words below.
They are all in Chapter Four.**

1 kind   ....
2 stupid   ....
3 cowardly   ....
4 dishonest   ....
5 wonderful   ....

Connecting sentences

Look how we can connect sentences in English.

- *The squire bought a ship **and then** he wrote to his friends.*
- *He sat by the fire **and** he drank some rum.*
- *Long John Silver is a cook **and** he knows many sailors.*
- *The pirates opened the sea-chest **but** they didn't find the map.*
- *Long John Silver moves easily about the ship, **but** he has only one leg.*
- *You can go visit the island **or** you can help me on the ship.*

3 **Fill in the gaps**

Read the text below. It is a simplified version of the beginning of Robert Louis Stevenson's book *In the South Seas*. He explains why he went to the islands of the South Pacific. Fill in the gaps with *or*, *but*, *and* or *and then*.

A few years ago I was very ill. In fact, I thought I was near the end of my life, **(0)** ......*and*............. I could only expect to spend my remaining days with nurses and doctors. A friend told me that I would get better in the South Seas. I thought about it **(1)** .... I decided to go. It was difficult for me to move, **(2)** .... people could carry me on and off ships. I left with my family on small ship called the *Casco* from San Francisco at the end of June 1888, **(3)** .... in January 1889 it arrived in Honolulu, Hawaii. There I thought: I can return home to my bed **(4)** .... I can continue my travels. I decided to visit the other parts of the South Pacific. I sailed on another ship, **(5)** .... reached the islands of Samoa in December 1889. At this time, I began to feel thankful toward these islands. I was stronger **(6)** .... I had new friends.

Time moves quickly for me. Now I am planning a new journey in the South Seas. Here I find life most pleasant and people most interesting. My situation is not unusual. In fact, many Europeans come, **(7)** .... few leave. This is one of the most attractive places in the world.

4 Summary

Read the summary of Chapters Three-Four and choose the right word or phrase.

The squire bought a ship in (**1**) **Liverpool/Bristol/London** called the *Hispaniola*. He also hired a man with (**2**) **a long scar/one leg/one arm** called Long John Silver as the ship's cook. Silver helped the squire find the sailors for the crew.

Soon after Jim and Dr Livesey arrived in Bristol, the *Hispaniola* began its voyage to Treasure Island.

The voyage was (**3**) **difficult/boring/pleasant**. The evening before they arrived at the island, Jim climbed into a (**4**) **boat/barrel/box** to get an apple. As he sat there he heard Long John talking to another sailor. Jim soon discovered that Long John was really a pirate and that he wanted the treasure for himself.

Just then the ship arrived at the island. To celebrate their arrival the squire and Dr Livesey went down in their cabin to drink some wine. Jim followed them and told them about Long John Silver's plans.

The next day the crew went to explore the island. Jim went with the them.

While Jim was alone exploring the island he heard some voices. It was Long John talking with a sailor named Tom. Just then they heard (**5**) **a shout/some laughter/a scream**. Long John told Tom that it was Allan. Tom began to leave because he did not want to help the pirates. As he went away Long John (**6**) **killed/shouted at/ran after** him.

Jim was terrified and ran away. As he ran he saw a strange man following him. This was Ben Gunn. He told Jim that he was a pirate and that he had been with Captain Flint when he (**7**) **fought the English/died/left the treasure on the island**. He also said that some other pirates had left him on the island three years earlier. However, Ben said that he would help Jim and his friends for (**8**) **some cheese/a boat/one thousand pounds**.

Just then they heard (**9**) **shouting/singing/guns**. Ben and Jim ran until they came to a fort with (**10**) **a pirate flag/a white flag/a Union Jack** waving over it.

Blackbeard and Black Bart

Perhaps the most famous pirate in history is Edward Teach, known as *Blackbeard* (about 1680-1718). Blackbeard was a very colourful character: he had a long black beard and long black hair; he wore a bright red coat and always carried a lot of guns and knives. He was born in Bristol, England, and went to sea on English privateer ships in the early eighteenth century. By his death in 1718, he had fourteen wives in different ports around Britain and the Caribbean. The last of these – Mary – was only sixteen years old. During his short career as a pirate between 1716 and 1718, he commanded two ships with a total of 250 British pirates. He successfully attacked French, Dutch, and Portuguese ships near the west coast of Africa.

During these years, he lived in the Bahamas and the Carolinas. When the governor of Virginia heard of Blackbeard's attacks on ships in the area, he sent Lieutenant Robert Maynard to find and kill him. He found Blackbeard's ship the *Adventure* in an inlet [1] in North Carolina on 21 November. He waited outside the inlet all night, planning to attack the *Adventure* by daylight. As the pirates waited for the battle, one said to Blackbeard, 'Did you tell your wife Mary where you buried the treasure?' Blackbeard replied, 'Only the Devil and I know where I buried the treasure!'

As soon as the sun rose, Blackbeard sailed out of the inlet, hoping to take Maynard by surprise. Maynard tried to follow and attack the

---

1. **inlet** : narrow strip of water that goes from the sea into the land.

The Capture of the Pirate Blackbeard, 1718 (18th century)
by Jean Léon Jerome Ferris. Notice Blackbeard's beard and weapons.

Adventure, but Blackbeard fired at Maynard's ship, the *HMS Ranger,* first, killing many of Maynard's men. He called out to Maynard, 'Damn you and your men! You are all cowards!' Then he told his pirates to fire the cannons again.

Maynard told all his crew to hide in the rooms below the deck. When the smoke cleared, Blackbeard saw that the deck of the *Ranger* was empty. He thought that all Maynard's crew had died in the battle, so he boarded the ship to loot [1] it. As soon as Blackbeard and his pirates were on board the *Ranger*, Maynard's men ran up onto the deck and attacked them. In the battle that followed, Maynard killed Blackbeard, then cut off his head and hung it from the *Ranger*'s mast. If Blackbeard really buried his treasure, no one ever found it. In fact, his reputation as the king of pirates is based more on his colourful character than on his success. Between 1716 and 1718 Blackbeard caught and looted thirty ships, but he never became a very rich man, as some other less famous pirates did.

Bartholomew Roberts (1682-1722), for example, is far less famous than Blackbeard even though his career as a pirate was far more successful. Roberts, who was known as *Black Bart*, attacked ships near the Americas and West Africa. He was the most successful pirate of all time: between 1719 and 1722 he captured over 470 ships. Roberts was born in Wales. He went to sea at the age of 13 and worked on British and Caribbean ships until 1719, when he was third mate aboard the slave ship the *Princess of London*. In June that year the *Princess of London* was attacked and captured by pirates on the Gold Coast of West Africa. Some of the crew of the *Princess of London* – including Roberts – were forced to join the pirates. Roberts was an excellent navigator, [2] and the pirates' captain, Howell Davis, realised that he was an important member of the crew. Roberts did not want to become a pirate, but he decided that the life of a pirate was better than the life of an honest seaman. As an honest seaman he had earned three pounds a month and had no chance of being promoted to captain. As a pirate, he had much greater opportunities.

1. **loot** : steal things.
2. **navigator** : a person who finds the best direction to travel.

Bartholomew Roberts (1724) by an unknown artist.
He looks a much more 'respectable' pirate than Blackbeard on page 59.

Six weeks after Roberts had reluctantly joined Davis's crew, Davis was killed and the crew elected Roberts captain of the ship because of his great skill as a navigator.

Soon afterwards, Roberts and his men sailed for Brazil, where they attacked and captured several ships. One of these – a Portuguese ship – contained 40,000 pieces of gold and jewellery made for the King of Portugal.

Roberts was not a typical pirate. He was always clean and well-dressed, and he did not drink alcohol. He loved music and hired musicians to play on his ships. He wrote a charter of laws for his crew. He was intelligent, just, and an excellent naval commander. Under his command, the pirates, who were usually drunken and disorganised, became a very effective fighting force.

By the spring of 1721, Black Bart was feared by all the honest seamen on the Atlantic and his attacks on ships had stopped trade in the West Indies. He therefore sailed to West Africa, where he and his pirates stayed at Cape Lopez to relax. Roberts read and listened to music, while the crew spent their money on drink and women.

Captain Chaloner Ogle, the captain of *HMS Swallow*, a British navy ship, saw Roberts's three pirate ships in the harbour at Cape Lopez. Knowing Black Bart's terrible reputation, Captain Ogle decided to attack. The attack took the pirates by surprise, and Captain Ogle captured one of their ships – the *Swallow* – then sailed away, and the surviving pirates thought that they were safe, so they returned to their pleasures at Cape Lopez. A few days later, the *Swallow* returned. Most of Roberts's crew was drunk when the *Swallow* fired the first shot, but Black Bart was not afraid. He dressed in his best clothes and went out on the deck to command his crew. The *Swallow* opened fire again, and Roberts was killed. After another two hours, the battle was over, and Captain Ogle had won. Only three pirates had been killed. The other 272 men of Roberts's crew were taken prisoner. Of these, seventy-five black crew members were sold into slavery by the Royal Navy and fifty-two of the others were hanged.

Captain Ogle was made a knight for his actions, and everyone admired him for defeating Black Bart. But perhaps Roberts was not unhappy about his early death. He had once said to his men 'The life of an honest seaman is a long and hard with little money and pleasure. The life of a pirate is short but happy.'

For each question choose the correct answer — A, B, C or D.

1   Blackbeard was famous for
    A ☐ his extravagant lifestyle and clothing.
    B ☐ courage and cruel nature.
    C ☐ skill as a commander.
    D ☐ skill as a navigator and fighter.

2   Blackbeard lost to Maynard because
    A ☐ Maynard tricked him.
    B ☐ Blackbeard became afraid.
    C ☐ Blackbeard had fewer men.
    D ☐ Maynard had more cannons.

3   Bartholomew Roberts became a pirate because
    A ☐ he wanted to travel and see the world.
    B ☐ he hated the captain of his ship.
    C ☐ he wanted to be a captain and have more money.
    D ☐ he liked the wild life of pirates.

4   The pirates chose Roberts as their new captain because
    A ☐ he was such a gentleman.
    B ☐ he knew how to navigate a ship very well.
    C ☐ he was a courageous fighter.
    D ☐ he knew where there was a lot of treasure.

5   Under Roberts' command the pirates
    A ☐ became more disciplined and better fighters.
    B ☐ drank more and fought less.
    C ☐ were treated very poorly.
    D ☐ never spent money on women.

6   Roberts thought that it was better to enjoy life than to
    A ☐ become famous.
    B ☐ have a lot of money.
    C ☐ worry about dying young.
    D ☐ win every battle.

Before you read

1 Jim returns to his friends

You will hear about Jim's arrival at the fort. For each question, fill in the missing information in the numbered space.

Jim and Ben arrive

Ben is certain that (**1**) .... are in the fort.

The fort was built by (**2**) ....

He knows this because he sees the (**3**) ....

Ben leaves

Ben will wait for Jim between (**4**) ....

Jim enters

Jim was happy when he saw that they had water, food and
(**5**) .... in the fort.

He became sad when he saw Redruth (**6**) ....

The pirates stopped firing the cannons and it became very
(**7**) ....

Jim told his friends about Allan, (**8**) ....

---

2 Reading pictures

Look at the picture on pages 66-67.

1   What is the condition of the men in the picture?

2   What do you think has happened?

Look at the picture on page 71.

1   Who's in the picture?

2   What is one of them carrying?

3   What do you think they want?

The Fort

Ben Gunn looked up at the flag and said, 'Your friends are in **there, Jim.'**

'Maybe the pirates are in there,' I replied.

'No! Pirates don't fly the Union Jack; they fly the Jolly Roger! Your friends are there, in the old fort that Flint built years ago. If they have food and guns, they'll be safe.'

I looked out to sea, where we had left the *Hispaniola* with the Union Jack flying from its mast. [1] Now the flag flying from the mast of the *Hispaniola* was the Jolly Roger! I knew then that Ben Gunn was right, so I cried out, 'Dr Livesey! Squire Trelawney! Are you in there? It's me! Jim!'

Just then I heard a loud noise and saw smoke going up from the *Hispaniola*. The pirates had fired [2] a cannon ball [3] at the fort. It flew over our heads and fell into the forest behind with a great explosion.

1. **mast** : long vertical pole to support sails and flags.
2. **fired** : shot.
3. **cannon ball** :

'I'm going!' cried Ben Gunn. 'Tell your captain what I told you. I'll be waiting for his answer tomorrow, between noon and six o'clock, at the place where you and I first met.'

Then he ran into the forest.

Another cannon ball exploded in the sand in front of me. Then the great wooden doors of the fort opened, and Dr Livesey cried out, 'Come quickly, Jim!'

I ran into the fort, and the doctor closed the doors behind me. Inside, I was surprised and happy to see the squire, Hunter,

Joyce, and another man called Gray. They had guns and food. They had fresh water because a little stream [1] ran through the centre of the fort. All this seemed too good to be true, until I saw the squire's old servant Redruth lying dead on the floor.

'Listen!' said the doctor. 'They've stopped firing cannon balls.'

We listened to the deep silence around the fort, then the squire said, 'They've used all the cannon balls. We didn't have

1. **stream** : small river.

many. Now, if they want to attack us, they must come to the fort with their guns. Let's sit around the fire. I want to hear about Jim's adventures and tell him about ours! Joyce — you stay by the window with your gun.'

I told them about Allan, Tom and Ben Gunn. They all cried out in horror when they heard about Allan and Tom. They listened with great interest to the strange story of Ben Gunn. Then the doctor told me what had happened to them since I left the *Hispaniola*.

'We heard that scream, Jim,' he said. 'We didn't know then that it was the pirates killing poor Allan, but we knew it was something bad. Six mutineers were left on the *Hispaniola* when the rest of you went to the island, and there were five of us. We wanted to throw the mutineers into the sea and sail away, but we couldn't leave you on the island, so we thought of another plan. The squire gave us all rifles [1] and we took the pirates by surprise. The squire and I pointed our rifles at them, while Redruth, Hunter, and Joyce filled two boats with food and guns. As we were getting into the boats, Gray said he wanted to come with us, to fight on our side and do his duty as an honest sailor. We agreed, and he got into one of the boats with us. The squire, still pointing his gun at the mutineers, said to them, "This is a hunting rifle, and I'm a good hunter. I can shoot an animal from a great distance and kill it. We are now going to the island. If you make any noise or try to send any kind of signal to Long John and your other pirate friends, I will shoot you dead." The pirates all agreed to be silent. Our plan was to get to the fort with food, guns, and the treasure map. We arrived on the island and carried

1. **rifles** :

The Fort

the food and guns up to the fort. Just as we were taking the last things from the boats, one of Long John's pirates saw us and ran to tell the others. They came running with their guns, and we were very fortunate to reach the fort before they could kill us all.' Here the doctor stopped for a moment and looked sadly over at Redruth's body lying on the floor.

The squire looked over there too, with tears in his eyes, 'Please forgive me, dear old Redruth!' he cried. 'Forgive me for taking you so far from home! It's all my fault that you're dead!'

'Nonsense!' said the doctor. 'Redruth died a hero's death. Now, where was I? Oh, yes: they killed poor Redruth, but we shot one of their men and wounded [1] two others. Once we were here in the fort, the squire opened his coat and took out the ship's Union Jack! He had taken it from the main mast and hidden it under his coat before we left the *Hispaniola*. We put the flag up over the fort to show you that we were here, Jim, and to show those mutineers that we are brave Englishmen and will fight to the end!'

We buried poor Redruth and said a prayer for him. Then we sat around the fire to eat our dinner and talk. We could hear the pirates shouting and singing in the distance, after an evening of drinking rum. The squire said, 'We have enough food to last for a little while, but not for long. Now there are only fifteen mutineers, and two of them are wounded. Let's stay in the fort and shoot any of them who come near.'

'Yes,' said the doctor, 'and maybe those we don't kill will die of too much rum and the bad climate of this island. The island is hot during the day but cold and damp [2] at night. In that climate it is easy to get ill. I have all the ship's medicines here with me.

1. **wounded** : injured.   2. **damp** : wet.

1111111111111111111111111111111111111111111111111111111111

11111111111111111111

Maybe the mutineers will all fall ill and die. Or, if some of them fall ill, maybe the others will decide to leave the island on the *Hispaniola*. Then we will be safe to wait here until an English ship comes to find us. In Bristol, they all know where the *Hispaniola* was going, and they know that we should be back home by August. At the end of August, they will send a ship to look for us.'

I was very tired and went to sleep as soon as I lay down that night. The next morning, I woke up to the sound of the squire's voice. He was looking out of the window with a look of great surprise on his big red face. 'It's Long John Silver!' he cried.

I ran to the window and looked out. In the grey light of a cold damp morning, I saw Long John Silver and another pirate named Morgan. Morgan was carrying a white flag.

The squire pointed his rifle at Long John and cried, 'Don't come any nearer, or I'll shoot!'

'This is a flag of truce,'[1] said Long John.

Morgan waved the white flag and said, 'Captain Silver wants to come into the fort to talk to you.'

The squire cried, 'Captain Silver?'

Long John laughed and said, 'Oh, the men have decided to make me captain, sir, because you abandoned the ship.'

The squire turned to us and said, 'Take your guns to the windows. We must watch in every direction. If you see any mutineers, shoot them. Doctor, you point your gun at Silver all the time that he is in the fort.' Then he turned back to the window and cried out, 'All right, Silver. You can come in.'

I opened the great wooden doors, and Long John Silver came in.

---

1. **truce** : when both sides in a war agree to stop fighting for a short time.

'Hello, Jim!' he cried in his old friendly voice, smiling as if nothing had changed since the days when he was ship's cook and I was cabin boy. 'Hello, Dr Livesey! Hello, Squire Trelawney! What a nice place you have here! You're all here together, safe and comfortable, like a happy family.'

'What do you want, Silver?' asked the squire.

'That was very clever of you, last night,' said Silver. 'We were all asleep, and one of you came and killed one of my men.'

I realised that Ben Gunn had gone to the pirate's camp in the night and killed one of them. Now there were only fourteen mutineers left.

The squire took out his pipe and lit it. 'Since you are smoking, sir, I will too,' said Long John, then he sat down beside the squire and lit his own pipe. For a few minutes the two men smoked in silence, then Silver said, 'We want that treasure map, and you want to get out of here alive. You have enough food here for a few days. What will happen after that? I'll tell you what will happen: you'll die. Either my men will shoot you when you come out of the fort to find food, or you'll stay in the fort with no food and die. But, if you give us the map, we won't kill you. We'll put the treasure on the *Hispaniola* and sail away. You can come with us, or you can stay here, and I'll speak to the captain of the next ship I see and tell him that you are on this island, in need of help. What do you say, sir?'

'I say no!' replied the squire. 'You are mutineers. We'll never give you the treasure map!'

Long John Silver looked angry. He stood up, took his crutch, and cried, 'Then we'll kill you all and take the map!' I opened the wooden doors, and he walked out into the cold morning.

Go back to the text

PET ① **Comprehension check**
For each question choose the correct answer — A, B, C or D.

1 The squire and Dr Livesey didn't sail away from the island because
   A ☐ they didn't have the treasure.
   B ☐ they wanted to capture Silver and bring him to England.
   C ☐ the weather was not good enough.
   D ☐ they didn't want to leave Jim behind.

2 Squire Trelawney felt responsible for Redruth's death because
   A ☐ Redruth didn't have a gun to protect himself.
   B ☐ he didn't send Redruth into the fort earlier.
   C ☐ they didn't stay on the ship where it was safe.
   D ☐ he brought Redruth from England on a dangerous adventure.

3 The doctor said that the pirates might leave the island because
   A ☐ it was impossible to find the treasure.
   B ☐ they did not want to become ill.
   C ☐ they did not want to be shot.
   D ☐ they were afraid of Ben Gunn.

4 Long John Silver said that he became captain because
   A ☐ his men captured the *Hispaniola*.
   B ☐ the squire left the ship without a captain.
   C ☐ he was more capable than the squire.
   D ☐ the crew did not like the squire.

5 Long John Silver came to the fort because
   A ☐ he wanted the treasure map.
   B ☐ he wanted Ben Gunn to stop killing his men.
   C ☐ he wanted medicine for his men.
   D ☐ he needed fresh water.

6 Until the squire refused his offer, Long John Silver was
   A ☐ respectful and pleasant.
   B ☐ nervous and suspicious.
   C ☐ arrogant and aggressive.
   D ☐ happy and satisfied.

73

PET ❷ The bad air of Treasure Island

Read the text below and choose the correct word for each space. For each question, mark the letter next to the correct word — A, B, C or D.

Treasure Island is dangerous place, but not just (0) ...B.............. of the pirates. Dr Livesey (1) .... that the wet climate could (2) .... people ill. The doctor does not know the real reason (3) .... wet, tropical climates are dangerous. He thinks the illness comes from the 'bad air'. Actually, it is malaria (this word (4) .... 'bad air' in Italian) that makes people ill. Malaria is a parasite that enters the human body when a mosquito bites you. The true origin of this disease was not (5) .... until 1880.

Scientists think that humans have always had malaria. The first written reference to malaria was in China about 5000 years (6) .... The Greek doctor Hippocrates described the symptoms of malaria (7) .... 400 BC.

Malaria has been eliminated from many parts of the world, (8) .... it is still a major problem. About 500 million people get this disease every year, and 2.5 million of these die. (9) .... health organisations are looking for new ways to fight (10) .... terrible disease.

0	**A** why	**B** because	**C** how	**D** what
1	**A** says	**B** tells	**C** speaks	**D** talks
2	**A** get	**B** make	**C** cause	**D** force
3	**A** this	**B** the	**C** that	**D** a
4	**A** means	**B** translates	**C** says	**D** stands
5	**A** seen	**B** learned	**C** discovered	**D** decided
6	**A** ago	**B** back	**C** then	**D** before
7	**A** in	**B** at	**C** on	**D** by
8	**A** but	**B** however	**C** and	**D** so
9	**A** Much	**B** Lots	**C** Great	**D** Many
10	**A** the	**B** that	**C** a	**D** this

3 Vocabulary

Find the opposites of the words in the box below. All the words in the box come from this chapter. There are seven words in the box that you do not need to use.

fortunate	poor	open	ill	now	loud	dead	stay	brave
honest	maybe	great	damp	happy	clever	cold	first

1 certainly .... 6 soft ....
2 last .... 7 alive ....
3 unlucky .... 8 closed ....
4 go .... 9 dry ....
5 stupid .... 10 warm ....

Before you read

1 Listening

Look at the six sentences. You will hear about the pirates' attack on the fort. Decide if each sentence is correct or incorrect. If it is correct, put a tick (✓) in the box under A for YES. If is not correct, put a tick (✓) in the box under B for NO.

      A   B
    Yes No

1 The squire thought that the pirates' attack would come soon. ☐ ☐
2 The attack came after three hours. ☐ ☐
3 They fired their guns in the general direction of the enemy. ☐ ☐
4 All of the pirates tried to get into the fort. ☐ ☐
5 The squire killed three pirates. ☐ ☐
6 A pirate killed Hunter. ☐ ☐

2 Reading pictures

Look at the picture on page 79.

1 Who's in the picture?   3 Where is he?
2 What's he doing?   4 Why do you think he is doing this?

75

Captain Jim Hawkins

When Long John Silver was gone, the squire said, 'They'll attack us soon. We must wait by the windows with our guns until they come. Jim, when the battle begins, you reload the guns.'[1]

We waited in silence for more than two hours, as the sun rose high in the sky, bright and hot. Then suddenly there was the sound of guns from the forest on three sides of the fort. We fired shot after shot from the north, east, and west windows, but we couldn't see the enemy. I went from man to man, reloading the guns as fast as I could. Then suddenly half the pirates came running out of the forest towards the fort. The other half stayed hidden behind the trees, firing at us when we appeared at the windows. The squire shot three pirates: two fell down dead and one ran off into the forest. But, by that time, four other pirates had got to the fort. Two of them climbed through a window while

---

1. **reload the guns** : make the guns ready for shooting again.

I was giving the doctor a loaded rifle. Another pirate, standing outside with his back to the wall of the fort, grabbed [1] the other end of Hunter's rifle and pulled it out through the window. He then shot Hunter, and he and the fourth pirate climbed through the window and over Hunter's dead body.

There were now four pirates in the fort. The air was full of smoke from the guns, so that it was difficult to see what was happening. I thought that the battle was lost and the pirates had won, but suddenly I saw the squire and the doctor in the middle of the room with their rifles. They shot three of the pirates one after another. The fourth pirate climbed back out of a window and ran into the forest. The gunfire from the forest stopped. It seemed that all the other pirates had run away.

'We've won! We've won!' I cried, but, looking around, I saw the price we had paid for our victory: Hunter and Joyce were dead on the ground.

'How many did we kill, Livesey?' asked the squire.

'Five of them,' the doctor replied.

'And they killed poor Joyce and Hunter,' said the squire sadly, but then he looked at the rest of us and smiled. 'But now there are only nine of them!'

We ate our lunch quickly; then the doctor took a sword and two guns and walked out into the forest to the north. He was going to find Ben Gunn. The fort was hot, and we hadn't buried the dead bodies yet. The place filled me with horror and disgust. I wanted to get away. I wanted to follow the doctor into the cool forest, but I knew that the squire wouldn't let me go. So I waited

---

1. **grabbed** : took hold of, quickly and tightly.

until no one was looking, then I took my gun and my knife, climbed out of one of the north windows, and ran into the forest.

My plan was to find Ben Gunn's boat. He had said it was on the east side of the island, behind a big white rock, so I turned east and ran through the forest until I reached the shore. It was late afternoon, and the sun was going down, when I found Ben Gunn's boat. I got in the boat and waited until dark, then I rowed down the east coast to the south, where the *Hispaniola* was anchored. [1] I rowed up to the ship and looked through the portholes. There was no one in the cabins. They were a terrible mess, with broken bottles and furniture. I heard two drunk [2] pirates fighting up on the deck. They were too busy to notice me, and they were the only men on the ship, so I took out my knife and cut the rope that was attached to its anchor. When the rope was cut, the *Hispaniola* moved on the waves and started to drift [3] away from the shore.

On shore, the pirates were shouting and singing, too drunk to notice that their ship was drifting away. I could see their fire and hear their voices.

Fifteen men on the Dead Man's Chest,
Yo-ho-ho, and a bottle of rum!

I tried to row the boat back to the eastern shore, but the tide [4] was against me. For hours, I rowed along the western shore, looking for a safe place to land, but I couldn't find one: that

1. **anchored** : prevented from moving by putting a heavy object (an anchor) into the water.
2. **drunk** : not able to act or speak normally because they had drunk too much alcohol.
3. **drift** : move here and there with no control over direction.
4. **tide** : the movement of the sea water.

shore was very rocky and dangerous. Finally, I fell asleep in the boat. When I woke up the sun was shining. The night before, I had rowed far away from the *Hispaniola*, but now I saw the great ship very close. It was moving when the wind filled its sails, but I couldn't see anyone on deck. 'Perhaps those two pirates are asleep, still drunk from last night,' I thought, 'or perhaps they killed each other when they were fighting!' I saw a rope hanging down from the deck of the ship into the water. Just then the wind filled the sails of the *Hispaniola*, and it came straight towards me. Just before the great ship hit the little boat and broke it to pieces, I grabbed the rope and climbed up.

When I got on deck, I saw two of the mutineers lying beside each other, covered in blood. One was dead. The other I recognised: his name was Israel Hands. He was very badly wounded. I walked up to him and said, 'Good morning, Mr Hands!'

Israel opened his eyes and looked up at me. 'Rum! Get me some rum!' he cried.

I went down into the cabin and got a bottle of rum, a cup of water, and some cheese, then I went back on deck. I gave the rum to Israel Hands then sat down beside him to drink my water and eat my cheese.

'What are you doing here?' asked Israel.

'Well, I'm now the captain of this ship,' I replied. 'There's no one else on board except you and him. You can't move, and he's dead, so I'm the captain now.'

'All right, Captain Hawkins,' said Israel. 'You've won. What do you plan to do?'

'I plan to take this ship to the northern harbour, where it can land even without an anchor,' I said.

'Let's make a deal,' [1] said Israel. 'You don't know how to control the ship, but I'll tell you what to do. If I do that you must bring me food and drink.'

'Agreed!' I said. 'But first I must take down that flag.' I ran to the main mast and took down the Jolly Roger.

Then Israel told me how to control the ship. The *Hispaniola* sailed with the wind up to the northern harbour. It was a beautiful harbour with a white sandy beach and clear blue water.

As I was looking over the side of the ship, at the beach, I heard a noise behind me. I turned and saw Israel coming towards me with a bloody knife in his hand. I pulled out my gun and pointed it at him. 'Drop that knife, Mr Hands,' I said, 'or I'll blow your brains out!' [2]

Israel threw the knife at me. It hit me in the shoulder. I did not intend to fire the gun, but, when the knife hit me, the gun went off, [3] and Israel Hands was shot in the chest. He fell overboard into the sea.

I pulled the knife out of my shoulder. Blood ran down my chest, but the wound wasn't serious or even very painful. The only pirate on the ship now was the dead one who had fought with Israel Hands. I went over to his body and pushed it overboard. The *Hispaniola* was now mine.

1. **deal** : agreement.
2. **blow your brains out** : shoot you in the head and kill you.
3. **went off** : fired a bullet.

Go back to the text

1 Comprehension check
Answer the following questions.

1 What was Jim's job during the battle with the pirates?
2 Why did Dr Livesey leave the fort?
3 Why did Jim want to leave the fort?
4 Who was left on the *Hispaniola*?
5 Why did Jim climb onto the *Hispaniola*?
6 Why did Israel Hands accept Jim as captain?
7 Where did Jim want to take the ship?
8 Why did Jim kill Israel Hands?

2 Summary
Put the sentences in the right order to make a summary of Chapters Five-Six, and then fill in the gaps with the correct word or words.

A ☐ The next morning Long John Silver came to the fort to talk to the squire. He said that if the squire gave him the (1) .... his men would not kill them.

B ☐ Then Jim tried to row his little boat to the eastern shore of the (2) .... In the end, it was too difficult and he was near the ship again.

C ☐ Ben Gunn and Jim arrived at the fort. They could see the (3) .... flying and so they knew that Jim's friends were inside.

D ☐ The squire refused the offer. Long John Silver became very angry and left.

E ☐ But before they arrived Hands tried to kill Jim and Jim shot Hands dead with his (4) ....

F ☐ They then waited for the pirates' attack. More than two hours later it came. At first the pirates were strong. But finally Jim and his friends (5) ....

G ☐ Just then the pirates fired the ship's (6) .... at the fort. Ben left and Jim entered the fort.

H ☐ Now Dr Livesey left to look for (**7**) .... Jim, too, decided to leave the fort.

I ☐ He climbed onto the ship and found Israel Hands and a (**8**) .... pirate. Hands was badly hurt.

J ☐ Jim and Hands made a (**9**) .... : Jim got him food and drink, and Hands helped Jim sail the ship to the northern harbour.

K ☐ He went to get Ben Gunn's boat. He rowed it out to the *Hispaniola*. He cut the rope attached to the (**10**) .... and the ship began to drift.

T: GRADE 4

3 **Speaking: sports**

Robert Louis Stevenson was proud of his knowledge of sailing. Stevenson also enjoyed hiking and canoeing when he was a young man. What about you? Using the following questions, prepare a short talk about you and sports.

- Do you do any sports?
- Which ones?
- How often do you do these sports?
- Describe an exciting moment.
- Which sports do you like to watch?
- How often do you watch them?
- Have you got a favourite team or sportsperson?

Now look at the pictures below. What are the names of these sports in English? Use a dictionary to help you. Compare these sports with regard to excitement, difficulty and danger.

1 rugby   **2** skiing   **3** football (american)   **4** cricket   **5** diving

A☐ B☐ C☐ D☐ E☐

PET ④ My first book

Look at the statements on page 87 about the writing of *Treasure Island*. Read the text below to decide if each statement is correct or incorrect. If it is correct, mark A. If it is not correct, mark B.

Treasure Island was not my first book. When I was a boy I wrote many stories, and when I was a young man I wrote some books about my travels. A couple of them were even published, but they were not at all successful. So, for the general public *Treasure Island* will always be my first book. It is the first book that they bought.

Now anybody can write a short story — a bad one, I mean — but a novel is different. You must have inspiration and good luck for a long time. When I saw a big novel I was always amazed. I did not think I could ever write one. But destiny helped me.

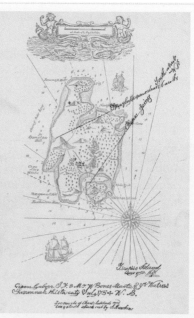

Stevenson drew a map of Treasure Island. This map then inspired him to write his novel.

One year, I went to live in a small house in Scotland with my father, my wife and her young son, Lloyd. The weather was always windy, cold and rainy. Lloyd began to paint pictures to pass the time. I too joined him. One day I made a detailed and colourful map of a place: I called it 'Treasure Island'. I know some people don't like maps, and I can't understand that. I can imagine many things when I look at one, and with this one, I immediately began to see pirates with swords in its imaginary woods.

Then, before I realized it, I was writing a story. I called it *The Sea Cook*. I wrote it to entertain Lloyd, but my father liked it too. In fact, he gave me many important details, like the contents of Billy Bones' chest.

Later I realized that my book had many ideas from other books by famous writers. The parrot, for example, comes from Robinson Crusoe and the skeleton is Edgar Allan Poe's idea. Still, every writer gets ideas from other writers. That's normal.

So, my book was a big success in my family. But how did it get published? Well, here too destiny helped me. A friend came to visit us, and this friend was the editor of a magazine. There was not much to do near our little house, and so I read him some of my story. He liked it, and, by chance, he was looking for stories for boys for a magazine.

Now I had to finish my first novel and finally, some time later in Switzerland, I finished it. My friend changed the title. I was finally a real novelist with a successful book. I know it is only a book for boys, but I am still proud of it and I still admire that clever pirate Long John Silver.

(This is the adaptation of an article that Stevenson wrote for the magazine *The Idler* in August 1894)

		A	B
1	*Treasure Island* is the first of Stevenson's books that the general public really liked.	☐	☐
2	Stevenson was always certain that he could write a novel.	☐	☐
3	Stevenson went to the small house in Scotland to write his first novel.	☐	☐
4	Lloyd drew a map of a place called 'Treasure Island'.	☐	☐
5	The map of 'Treasure Island' inspired Stevenson to write *Treasure Island*.	☐	☐
6	Stevenson's father gave him many ideas for *Treasure Island*.	☐	☐
7	Stevenson thinks it is bad to take ideas from other writers.	☐	☐
8	Stevenson read his friend the editor part of his book to entertain him.	☐	☐
9	*Treasure Island* was not written for adults.	☐	☐

Islands of the Imagination

The United Nations Convention on the Law of the Sea says that 'An island is a naturally formed area of land surrounded by water.' Of course, there are not just islands in the seas of world, there are also islands in lakes... and in the imagination.

An island of the imagination is often a kind of special world with its own rules and ways.

Stevenson's Treasure Island, for example, is a world of nightmare. Its vegetation has a horrible grey colour and its air brings sickness. It also hides a treasure. But to get this treasure young Jim Hawkins must also discover the worst aspects [1] of human nature. This island in some part of the world – maybe the Caribbean, but the author never tells us – is also the world where Jim becomes a man. But for Jim Treasure Island will always be the place of his worst dreams.

The writer J.M. Barrie (1860-1937), a friend of Stevenson's, made Treasure Island into a fairyland island that he called Neverland. Here, too, there is a little boy who fights pirates. But this little boy, unlike Jim, never grows up. His name is Peter Pan, and his enemy is a fierce pirate called Captain Hook. Hook, Barrie tells us, is the only man that Long John Silver was ever afraid of. This island, then, is not a place where a boy grows up, but a world of permanent childhood.

Another imaginary island that has fascinated the world is the island described so precisely in the novel *Robinson Crusoe* (1719) by Daniel Defoe (1660-1731). Defoe says that this island is somewhere off the coast of South America. Crusoe was shipwrecked there for 28 years.

---

1. **aspects** : characteristics, parts.

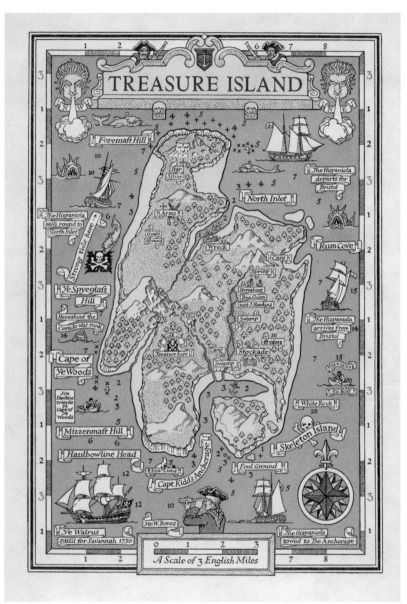

The map of Treasure Island (by Monro S. Orr)
from a 1937 edition of *Treasure Island*.

Crusoe, unlike Ben Gunn, does not go mad. He creates, according to many critics, a typical British colony in miniature.

But humans have always imagined distant islands representing both hope and fear. Many ancient cultures had legends about 'islands of the blessed': islands of joy where the dead go. The Celts, for example, told stories about the island of Avalon. They said that it was located somewhere in the British Isles. The legendary King Arthur was taken there at his death. Some stories also say that Jesus visited Avalon and founded the first church in Britain. Similarly, Irish mythology describes the blessed island of Tír na nÓg, which is located 'far to the west'. Sickness and death do not exist here, only joy.

Then philosophers and writers began to use the idea of islands of joy to illustrate their ideas for a better world. The Greek philosopher Plato (472-347 BCE) described the society of the legendary island of Atlantis to present his ideas of government. Plato's Atlantis then inspired the English philosopher and lawyer Thomas More (1478-1535), who wrote about an island called Utopia ('utopia' can mean either 'no place' or 'good place' in Greek). More located Utopia in the New World; he had just read about the explorations of Amerigo Vespucci (1454-1512). Even today, nobody knows for certain if Utopia represents More's ideal world or his ironic version of the real world.

Another famous writer who imagined fantastic islands in order to criticise our real world was Jonathan Swift (1667-1745). In his novel *Gulliver's Travels* (1726) Lilliput and Blefuscu are small islands in the South Indian Ocean. They are inhabited by men less than 12 centimetres high. The tiny men of these two islands fight each other because they disagree about how to break and eat an egg: from the big end or from the small end? Swift also imagined a flying island called Laputa. This island was created by scientists, who use

Gulliver and the island of Laputa (19th century) by an unknown French artist.

magnetic forces to move it. Its inhabitants are interested in mathematics, astronomy and technology, but they know little about the real world. Their thoughts and ideas move around in different directions like their flying island.

These island utopias have continued to inspire writers. More recently, H. G. Wells – one of the creators of modern science fiction –

imagined an island of biological horrors. In his 1896 novel *The Island of Dr Moreau*, the narrator, Edward Prendick, is shipwrecked on an island. He discovers that Dr Moreau has built his laboratory there, and has created horrible creatures that are half-man and half-beast.

Of course, imaginary islands have not just appeared in books. Films offer a vast selection of positive and negative utopias. In the 1993 film *Jurassic Park* the island of Isla Nublar has been planned as a kind of paradise – a world where time has stopped, a world where dinosaurs live. But this paradise soon turns into a place of nightmare.

Even more recently, Stevenson's *Treasure Island* itself inspired the skull-shaped Isla de Muerta of the 2003 film *Pirates of the Caribbean: The Curse of the Black Pearl*. The film's main character, a pirate named Jack Sparrow (certainly inspired by the immoral and charming Long John Silver), says that Isla de Muerta is 'an isle of the dead which cannot be found except by those who already know where it is.'

Nowadays we often visit worlds imagined for computers. The creators of role-playing video games have also been inspired by islands. The very popular 1990 video game *The Secret of Monkey Island* has as its hero a young man named Guybrush Threepwood. Interestingly, Guybrush wants to become a pirate and he ends up on a Caribbean island called Mêlée.

Some authors of role-playing video games have even gone back to the islands of ancient legends – they have created fantastic islands with distinctive cultures and societies. The famous 2001 *Final Fantasy X* presents a land called Spira. Spira, which reflects the geography of Southeast Asia, includes numerous islands with wonderful names like Besaid and Kilika.

So, from ancient myth to today's video games, imaginary islands continue to fascinate us.

Johnny Depp as Captain Jack Sparrow in *Pirates of the Caribbean: The Curse of the Black Pearl* (2003). Depp based his look on the rock star Keith Richards of the Rolling Stones, but his clothes are also historical: compare him with the picture of Blackbeard on page 59.

1 Comprehension check

Answer the questions.

1 What kind of special world is Treasure Island?
2 What is the name of the little boy who lives on Neverland?
3 How is Neverland like Stevenson's Treasure Island?
4 How is it different?
5 Where is Robinson Crusoe's island located?
6 What kind of world does Crusoe create on this island?
7 What is the name of Thomas More's island?
8 What are the two possible meanings of the name of that island?
9 Where is Avalon? Who founded a church there?
10 What kind of place is Isla Nublar?
11 What real part of the world inspired the land of Spira?

Before you read

1 Listening

PET

You will hear about Jim's return to the fort. For each question, put a tick (✓) in the correct box.

1 Jim thinks that the squire will be angry with him because
  A ☐ he left the fort.
  B ☐ he took Ben Gunn's boat.
  C ☐ he left the *Hispaniola*.

2 When Jim arrived in the fort he decided to
  A ☐ sleep.
  B ☐ wake everybody up.
  C ☐ wake up just the squire.

3 Then Jim heard a voice. It was
  A ☐ Morgan.
  B ☐ the parrot.
  C ☐ Long John Silver.

4 At first, he thought that his friends were dead because
  A ☐ the pirates were in the fort.
  B ☐ there weren't any prisoners.
  C ☐ he could not see well in the light of the torch.

5 When Long John Silver spoke to Jim he sounded
  A ☐ happy to see him.
  B ☐ angry.
  C ☐ a little bit confused.

2 Reading pictures

Look at the picture on page 97.

1 Who has Jim found in the fort?

Look at the picture on page 101.

2 Who has come to see the pirates?
3 Why do you think he has come?
4 How does he look at Jim?
5 Why do you think he looks at him in this way.

Back to the Fort

I climbed down the rope onto the beach and ran into the forest. I wanted to get back to the fort as soon as possible, to tell my friends about my adventures and enjoy their looks of amazement and admiration. 'Perhaps,' I thought, 'the squire will be angry with me for running away, but I hope when he hears that I have captured the *Hispaniola* he will forget his anger!' With these happy thoughts I went through the forest as the sun went down and the moon rose in the night sky. When I got to the fort it was very late. I could see no lights except the fire, and the only sounds were the sounds of men snoring. [1]

I went up to a window and climbed in quietly. 'I'll just go to bed,' I thought. 'Then, in the morning, they'll all be surprised to see me.'

Just then there was a loud squawk and a voice cried, 'Pieces of eight! Pieces of eight!'

---

1. **snoring** : making a loud noise while breathing in sleep.

Suddenly I saw Long John Silver by the fire. The parrot was on his shoulder. He put a torch into the fire. By the light of the torch, I saw six mutineers but no prisoners. I thought, 'They've killed my friends!' Of the mutineers, Morgan and Merry were wounded, and Dick had the fever. They all looked tired and ill. On the floor by the wall, the seventh mutineer, one who had been wounded, was now lying dead.

'Hello, Jim!' said Long John. 'Have you come to visit us? How nice!' His voice was the same kind friendly voice as always, but his face was pale and serious, and his clothes were torn and dirty. He sat down and lit his pipe.

'I knew you were a clever boy, Jim, when I first met you,' said Long John. 'But I had no idea how clever you were.'

The other pirates pointed their guns at me. I sat by the wall in silence, looking angrily at Long John Silver, but I was really very sad and afraid.

'I've always liked you, my boy,' said Long John, 'I always wanted you to join up with me and be a pirate. You remind me of myself when I was young: I was clever and brave and handsome, just like you! Well, now you have no choice. You must join up with old Long John Silver and be a pirate, because your friends are angry with you for running away. They won't take you back, Jim. The doctor came to our camp with a white flag of truce this morning. He told us that the ship was gone. The men were sleeping after their rum, and no one had seen that the harbour was empty. The doctor and I made a deal: he left me this fort with all its food and guns, and I let him and the others go without trying to shoot them. "How many are left of you?" I asked him, and he said to me, "There are only three of us. I don't

know where that boy is, and I don't care!" So you see, Jim, you have no choice.'

I was happy to hear that my friends were still alive.

'I'm not afraid of you, Long John Silver,' I cried. 'You've lost the treasure, the ship, and most of your men, and I'm the one responsible: I stole the captain's treasure map; I stole your ship and put it where you'll never find it; and I killed Israel Hands. You can kill me now, or you can make a deal with me. If you let me live, I will testify for you in court[1] and save you from the gallows!'[2]

'Let's kill him!' cried Merry.

Long John turned to him angrily and cried, 'Are you the captain here? Do you want to fight with me? If you touch that boy, I'll kill you! That boy behaves more like a man than any one of you!'

Merry fell silent and sat down again. The other pirates went and sat beside him, and they started whispering[3] to each other. Every few minutes, one of them looked over at Long John Silver. Then Dick took out his Bible and a knife. He always carried his Bible with him, even when he was a mutineer. Dick was a very religious man, before he got into bad company on the *Hispaniola*. I tried to see what Dick was doing with the knife and the Bible, but then Merry stood between us, and I couldn't see him any more.

Long John smoked his pipe in silence for a while then he whispered to me, 'These men will try to kill me, and they'll try to kill you too. Let's make a deal: I'll protect you as much as

---

1. **testify for you in court** : tell the judge that you are innocent.
2. **gallows** : the place where criminals were executed by hanging.
3. **whispering** : speaking very quietly.

possible, and you'll testify for me in court if we get back to England. You speak so well, Jim, and you sound so clever and brave and honest that I'm sure any judge will believe what you say.'

'All right,' I said. 'I'll do what I can to help you.'

'When I saw that the ship was gone,' said Long John, 'I knew it was all over. I know you have that ship hidden safe somewhere. Well, I'm on the squire's side now. I'm not a pirate any more, Jim. Do you want a drink of rum?'

'No, thank you,' I said.

He poured himself a glass of rum, then he said, 'There's just one thing I don't understand. Why did the doctor give me the treasure map?'

I looked at him in amazement.

Just then, Dick came over to Long John Silver.

'What do you want?' asked Long John.

Dick stood there nervously.

'Come on!' said Long John. 'You don't need to be afraid of me.'

Dick gave something to him. It was a piece of paper, cut into a circle. Dick had cut it out of his Bible and blackened one side with a piece of wood from the fire. Long John looked at it and said, 'Ah! The Black Spot! I thought so. Why are you giving me the Black Spot?'

Dick replied, 'Because you're no good as a captain. You've lost the ship, and most of your men are dead! And you made a deal with the enemy and let them go!'

'Yes. Why do you think I did that?' cried Long John. 'I did it because you all need the doctor's help. The doctor said he would come here every morning to examine you and give you medicine.

And there was another reason too.' Then he took the treasure map and threw it on the floor. 'That's why! But you say I'm no good as a captain. All right! Choose someone else to be your captain! I'm tired of you all!'

The pirates all cried out together, 'No! We want you to be the captain! We want Long John Silver!'

'Well, then,' said Long John. 'Let's be friends again. I'll be your captain because I'm the best man among you. Let's have a drink of rum and go to bed.'

I lay awake for a long time that night. I thought about the man I had killed. I thought about the dangerous situation I was in. But most of all, I thought about Long John Silver. I knew that he was a bad man, but I felt sorry for him. I worried about the dangerous game he was playing. How could he be captain of the mutineers and be on the squire's side at the same time?

The next morning, I was awoken by a voice calling from outside the fort. I ran to the window and saw the doctor standing outside in the grey morning light.

'Hello, Dr Livesey!' cried Long John, and he let the doctor into the fort. When he saw me, the doctor stopped and stared [1] in amazement. Then he went to one of the wounded men and started his work, putting medicine on the wound and asking the man how he felt. When he had examined all the sick men, he said, 'I want to talk to that boy before I go.'

'Of course,' said Long John. He opened the doors and the three of us went outside. Long John turned to me and said, 'Don't try to run away. If you run away, those pirates will kill me.'

---

1. **stared** : looked for a long time.

'I won't.'

Then Long John turned to the doctor and whispered, 'I'm on your side now, although those pirates don't know it. You can talk to the boy, but then he must come back into the fort.'

'Why, John,' replied the doctor. 'You're not afraid, are you?'

'No!' cried Long John. 'I'm not afraid of those five idiots, but I'm afraid of the gallows! I know that you're a good man. Please remember the good things I did as well as the bad. For example, allowing you to talk to Jim now.'

Long John walked back into the fort and closed the doors.

The doctor said, 'Why did you run away, Jim? We needed your help.'

I started to cry. 'I'm sorry!' I said. 'I know what I did was wrong. I'll probably die now, because of it. Those pirates want to kill me, but Long John won't let them.'

'Jim, let's run now, into the forest.'

'No. I told Long John I wouldn't run away. I'm not afraid to die, but I'm afraid that the pirates might force me to tell them where the ship is. I stole the ship and hid it in the northern harbour.'

'The ship! Jim, you've saved our lives, and we'll save yours!' Then the doors of the fort opened and Long John came out again. 'Silver,' said the doctor. 'Don't go looking for that treasure. It's dangerous. I can't tell you more than that.'

'I must look for the treasure, sir. If I don't, those pirates will kill me.'

'Well, I'll try to help you. Please take good care of Jim. If you do, I'll speak for you in court when we get back to England. I'll do everything I can, as an honest man, to save you from the gallows.'

Go back to the text

1 **Comprehension check**

Match the phrases in column A with those in column B to make complete sentences. There are three phrases in column B that you do not need to use.

A

1 ☐ The doctor was angry with Jim
2 ☐ The doctor was happy with Jim
3 ☐ Jim must become a pirate, said Long John Silver
4 ☐ The doctor came to the fort
5 ☐ Jim was happy when he heard that his friends didn't want him anymore
6 ☐ The pirates didn't kill Jim
7 ☐ The pirates didn't choose another captain
8 ☐ Jim did not run away with the doctor
9 ☐ Long John Silver decided to become friends with Jim

B

A because the pirates were ill.
B because that meant that they were still alive.
C because he captured the *Hispaniola*.
D because Jim reminded him of himself when he was a boy.
E because Long John showed them that he had the treasure map.
F because he refused to break his promise to Long John Silver.
G because he ran away from his friends and they needed his help.
H because Long John Silver stopped them.
I because he was afraid of the gallows.
J because his friends don't want him anymore.
K because he was looking for Jim.
L because he promised Long John Silver that he wouldn't leave him.

PET ② The original Long John Silver

Look at the statements below about the original Long John Silver. Read the text to decide if each statement is correct or incorrect. If it is correct, mark A. If it is not correct, mark B.

Some people think the real Treasure Island is one of the Virgin Islands in the Caribbean. Others have suggested that the original island was in a small lake in a park near Stevenson's childhood home. After all, a little island in a little lake looks big to an imaginative little boy. However, Stevenson himself said that it was entirely the product of his own imagination. But the idea for Ben Gunn comes from the fictional character Robinson Crusoe of the book of the same name.

But what about the charismatic Long John Silver? Stevenson wrote that he based this character on a real person. A cruel pirate? A clever criminal? Actually, the original for the pirate with one leg and

William Henley.
Writer and editor.

a parrot on his shoulder was a poet and editor. His name was William Henley (1849-1903), and he was Stevenson's friend. He was a large, friendly and very intelligent man with a big red beard and a strong personality. He enjoyed having fun, arguing and drinking whisky. Henley, though, had only one foot. Stevenson said that Henley gave him the idea for a character with a physical handicap that ruled and was feared by his voice alone. But Stevenson also said that in no other way was Silver like his friend.

A   B

1   The original Treasure Island is actually an island in a city park. ☐ ☐

2   Ben Gunn was a character in the book *Robinson Crusoe*. ☐ ☐

3   William Henley wrote poems about criminals. ☐ ☐

4   Henley was a calm man.

5   Both Long John Silver and Henley had strong personalities and a physical problem. ☐ ☐

6   Stevenson was sometimes afraid of Henley. ☐ ☐

3 Writing – help your enemies
In about 100 words give your opinion of Dr Livesey. Include the following information:

- How he treats Billy Bones
- What he does when the pirates become ill
- Your opinion of his actions

You can begin like this:

Dr Livesey is not the hero of the book 'Treasure Island', but he is certainly a courageous man. In the beginning of the book he...

Before you read

1 Listening

You will hear about how Long John Silver acts with Jim and the pirates. For each question, fill in the missing information in the numbered space.

Long John – everybody's friend and leader

Long John to Jim

Long John thanks Jim because he did not (**1**) ....

Long John now considers Jim his (**2**) ....

Long John to the pirates

He is a good captain because he obtained the
(**3**) ....

The *Hispaniola* will take them off (**4**) ....

Jim's reaction

Jim is worried because he knows that Long John is a
(**5**) .... man.

The pirates' reaction

The pirates were now (**6**) ....

After the treasure

Once they began walking Jim became (**7**) .... of
Long John.

2 Reading pictures

Look at the picture on page 111.

1 Who is in this picture?

2 What are they doing?

3 The skeleton was left there for a reason. Why, do you think?

The Treasure Hunt

As we walked back into the fort, Long John whispered to me, 'You're a good boy, Jim. You could have run away just now, but you didn't. I thank you for that. I won't forget it. We're partners now. We're in this together.'

Then he went up to the pirates and said, 'You're lucky to have me for a captain! I got the treasure map for you, and now I know that they have the ship. I don't know where it is yet, but we'll find it. We have the boats, and we can row around the island until we find the *Hispaniola*. When we've got the treasure, we'll put it in the ship, and we'll sail away from this terrible island! Our enemies won't attack us, because we have a hostage — young Jim Hawkins here.'

The pirates looked happy now, but I was worried. Long John Silver was a bad man, and he would do anything to get the treasure and his freedom. I was also worried about my friends. I didn't understand why they had left the fort and given the treasure map to Silver. And why did Dr Livesey say that it would be dangerous to hunt for the treasure?

'Come on, men,' cried Long John. 'We've got the map. Let's go and find this treasure!'

We left the fort and walked to the boats on the south shore. Then we rowed the boats a little way up the west coast. We got out of the boats and walked through the forest towards the place in the south-west part of the island that was marked on the map with a red cross. Long John and his men carried guns and swords. As we walked, Long John looked at me several times. He didn't look kind or friendly now. I was frightened of him. I knew he was thinking about the treasure and how to escape with it.

It was a very long walk and the sun was hot. As we got close to the place, Morgan cried out in fear and surprise. We all ran to him to see what he had found. Under a pine tree lay the skeleton of a man. The skeleton was lying in a very strange position, with its arms above its head.

Long John looked at the skeleton. 'I think old John Flint was mad!' he said. 'It makes me feel cold to think about him. This must be one of the six men who came with him onto this island to bury the treasure. He killed them all! And he put this one into this strange position for a reason: the skeleton is pointing to the place where the treasure is buried!'

'I'm glad old Flint is dead!' said Morgan, looking around afraid. 'I was there when he died, with Billy Bones and Darby McGraw and Ben Gunn. Flint had a private talk with Bill. Then he started singing his old song — "Fifteen men". Then, just before he died, he asked Darby to get him some rum. His face was blue. I was afraid to look at him!'

'Come on, men! There's nothing to be afraid of!' cried Long John in a happy voice. 'Old Flint is dead, and I don't believe in ghosts. Let's go and get that treasure!'

Just then, a voice came out of the forest, singing the song they knew so well:

Fifteen men on the Dead Man's Chest,
Yo-ho-ho, and a bottle of rum!

The pirates all went pale with fear. Morgan cried, 'It's old Flint's ghost! He's come to kill us!'

'Nonsense!' cried Long John. 'That's no ghost! That's someone trying to frighten us. I don't know who he is, but I know he's a living man. Come on! Let's go and find the treasure!'

Long John took out the map and read out the instructions written on the back of it: 'Go to the tallest tree in the area. From that point you can see the top of Spyglass Hill and you can also see Skeleton Island.' Then he turned to the pirates and said, 'All we have to do is find that tree and dig for the treasure.'

But then we heard the voice from the forest again: 'Darby McGraw! Darby McGraw! Get me some rum!'

The pirates stood still, staring around with frightened eyes.

'That's strange,' said Long John. 'No one on this island except us knows Flint's last words. But I'm not afraid. I wasn't afraid of Flint when he was alive, and I'm not afraid of him now that he's dead! Still, that voice didn't sound like Flint, but I know that voice from somewhere...' He thought for a moment and then he cried, 'It's Ben Gunn!'

'Yes! You're right!' cried Merry. 'It's Ben Gunn's voice!'

'But what's Ben Gunn doing here?' asked Dick.

'I don't know,' replied Long John, 'and I don't care. Ben Gunn doesn't frighten me, dead or alive!'

The pirates looked much happier now. They walked along, talking to each other and laughing. Finally, we saw a very tall tree in the distance.

'That's it!' cried Long John, and we all ran to the tree, but then we stopped and stared in horror. Below the tree was a deep hole in the ground. The treasure was gone!

All six men stood still in shock, staring at the hole. Then Long John gave me one of his guns and whispered in his old friendly voice, 'Take that, Jim. They'll attack us now.'

I whispered back to him, 'So you've changed sides again!'

Long John and I were standing on one side of the hole, and the five pirates were standing on the other. Merry turned to the others and said, 'There's five of us and only two of them! And they're just a one-legged man and a boy! It's Silver's fault that we're all dying here on this miserable island! He knew there was no treasure! Let's kill them!'

Just then, the squire, the doctor, Gray and Ben Gunn ran out of the forest, firing their rifles. Merry and Morgan were shot dead and fell into the hole. The other three mutineers ran away.

'Quick!' cried the doctor. 'This way is shorter! We'll get to the boats before they do!'

We ran to the shore. The doctor shot big holes [1] in the bottom of one of the boats, and we all got into the other and rowed away before the three pirates got to the shore. As we rowed up the western coast, the doctor told us what had happened to them since I ran away from the fort.

---

1. **holes** : openings.

'I met Ben Gunn in the forest,' said the doctor, 'and he told me that he had found the treasure and moved it to a safe place. I went to the pirates' camp to talk to Long John. On the way there, I saw that the ship was gone. So I made a deal with Long John. The map was no use now, but he didn't know that, so I gave him the map and the fort, and we all left with Ben Gunn. Ben took us to a cave on the north of the island. He had hidden the treasure there. We're going there now.'

We rowed into the northern harbour, where the *Hispaniola* was drifting on the tide. Gray climbed the rope and got onto the deck of the ship. We left him there to guard it. Two miles further along the coast, we stopped the boat and got out. On the cliff above us, we saw Ben Gunn's cave. The squire was standing outside it, waving to us. When he saw Long John, he cried, 'You terrible man! You mutineer! It's all your fault that so many men have died! The doctor says that I can't speak against you in court. Well, then, I won't. But it makes me angry!'

'Thank you, sir,' said Long John.

We followed the squire into the cave. It was large with a sandy floor and a little stream of fresh water running through it. In the back of the cave was a great pile of coins and bars of gold. There were coins from England, France, Spain, Portugal and many other countries. Here, finally, was Flint's treasure. How many men had died looking for it!

Go back to the text

PET ❶ Comprehension check

For each question, choose the correct answer — A, B, C or D.

1 Long John Silver complimented Jim because
   A ☐ he was courageous.
   B ☐ he didn't go with Dr Livesey.
   C ☐ he decided to be his partner.
   D ☐ Jim wanted to help him find the treasure.

2 Long John said that he kept Jim alive because
   A ☐ he was a form of protection for them.
   B ☐ he knew where the treasure was.
   C ☐ he knew where the ship was.
   D ☐ he was now his partner.

3 Jim thought Long John would do anything to get the treasure because
   A ☐ he went to look for the treasure after Dr Livesey said it was dangerous.
   B ☐ he had lost many of his men, but he went to look for it anyway.
   C ☐ he continued to be the pirates' leader and also acted like Jim's friend.
   D ☐ he was without a ship but he still went to look for the treasure.

4 Flint placed the skeleton in a particular position to
   A ☐ frighten people looking for the treasure.
   B ☐ show his men that he was dangerous.
   C ☐ help him find the treasure again.
   D ☐ help Long John find the treasure.

5 When Long John first heard a voice singing 'Fifteen men...' he was convinced that it was
   A ☐ a ghost.
   B ☐ Ben Gunn.
   C ☐ Dr Livesey.
   D ☐ a living person.

2 Word square

Find the words in the three different categories. Then find these same words in the word square below.

The Law

- If a man is condemned to die, he goes to the g _ _ _ _ _ _
- The place where legal decisions about criminals are made: _ _ _ _ t
- To say something about somebody accused of a crime: t _ _ _ _ _ _
- The person who decides if a person has or has not done a crime: _ _ _ g _

Battles

- To make a gun ready to fire again: r _ _ _ _ _
- A long gun: _ _ f _ _
- A building to protect against the attack of an enemy: _ _ r _
- A weapon like a big knife: s _ _ _ _

Ships and the sea

The floor on a ship: d e c k

The large pieces of cloth that catch the wind to move a ship: s a i l s

The daily rising and falling of the sea: t i d e

- A big, heavy hook used to hold a ship in one place: a _ _ _ _ _
- The round windows of a ship: _ _ _ _ h _ _ _
- To be moved in different directions by the water: d _ _ _ _
- The part of the land next to the sea: _ h _ _ _

S	F	E	E	L	I	N	J	U	D	G	E	B	I	G
V	H	S	D	E	C	K	R	W	H	E	N	B	P	I
O	W	O	T	D	O	T	H	I	N	G	H	O	O	P
X	G	A	R	C	S	H	O	S	F	T	H	T	L	O
W	U	A	M	E	N	A	F	U	C	L	A	I	T	R
A	S	S	L	U	C	M	I	D	I	C	E	D	R	T
N	W	L	E	L	C	H	E	L	C	U	M	E	Y	H
F	O	R	T	I	O	N	S	I	S	W	G	H	F	O
T	R	K	I	N	U	W	Z	O	O	L	E	G	A	L
A	D	Q	U	I	R	T	S	D	R	I	F	T	R	E
L	A	G	O	D	T	B	U	T	B	R	A	G	M	S
K	C	O	N	Q	U	E	T	E	S	T	I	F	Y	F
I	R	E	L	O	A	D	F	V	G	A	M	X	R	I
G	L	O	S	S	P	U	L	A	N	C	H	O	R	S

INTERNET PROJECT

A Great Illustrator

Go to the Internet and go to www.blackcat-cideb.com or www.cideb.it.
Insert the title or part of the title of the book into our search engine.
Open the page to *Treasure Island*. Click on the Internet project link.
Scroll down the page until you find the title of this book and click on
the relevant link for this project.

In 2001 Billy Bones appeared on a United States postage stamp. The
United States did not wish to honour a drunken old pirate: it wished to
honour a great American illustrator, N. C. Wyeth.

▶ When did Wyeth live?

▶ Where did he live?

▶ Which museum has the best collection of his works?

▶ What are the names of his son and grandson? Why are they
famous?

▶ Download some of his illustrations that you like. Present them to the
class.

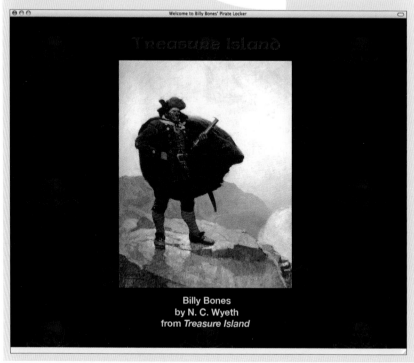

Billy Bones
by N. C. Wyeth
from *Treasure Island*

Before you read

PET ❶ **Listening**

You will hear about how Jim and his friends left the island. For each question, put a tick (✓) in the correct box.

1 They had their dinner
   A ☐ on the ship.
   B ☐ in the cave.
   C ☐ by the sea.

2 Long John Silver seemed to be
   A ☐ sad.
   B ☐ angry.
   C ☐ happy.

3 Jim thinks that the pirates did not attack because they
   A ☐ had enough fighting.
   B ☐ were too afraid to fight.
   C ☐ were planning their final attack.

4 They left the pirates on the island because
   A ☐ they were too dangerous to bring on the ship.
   B ☐ they wanted to punish them.
   C ☐ they didn't know where the pirates were.

5 When the pirates saw the *Hispaniola* leaving they
   A ☐ tried to reach the ship in a boat.
   B ☐ tried to shoot Jim and his friends.
   C ☐ asked them urgently not to go without them.

The Voyage Home

 www.blackcat-cideb.com

That night we cooked goat's meat on the fire and drank wine from the *Hispaniola*. I was happy to be with my friends again. Long John Silver smiled and poured wine for everyone.

The next morning we started to move the treasure from the cave to the *Hispaniola*. We didn't see the mutineers. They were probably tired of fighting now. It took two days to get all that treasure onto the ship, but finally it was done. On the third day we left some food, guns, and medicines on the beach for the three pirates. We had decided to leave them on the island: it wasn't safe to take them with us on the ship.

We then went on board the *Hispaniola* and sailed out of the northern harbour. Suddenly we saw them standing on a cliff, waving and calling out to us, 'Please, please, don't leave us here to die!'

The doctor cried out, 'We've left you food, guns, and medicine on the beach! Goodbye!'

We sailed to the nearest port in South America. When we arrived on land, we were welcomed by the friendly, smiling people. They sold us fruit and vegetables and showed us the town.

@ ENI

CHAPTER NINE

The streets were full of light and music! So different from the miserable island we had just left. We spent the night in the town, leaving Ben Gunn to guard the ship. When we returned the next morning, Ben said, 'Silver's gone! He escaped on a boat last night. He took a bag of coins with him. I'm not sorry! We weren't safe with Long John Silver on board!'

The next day we hired some sailors from the town and set sail for England. We each got a part of the treasure. I went back to the Admiral Benbow and lived happily with my mother. We hired some people to help us in the inn, so we don't have to work so hard any more. The squire is living well on his part of the treasure in our old village near Bristol. Gray used his money well: he studied his profession and became first mate on a fine ship. He is now married and the father of a family. Ben Gunn got one thousand pounds and spent it in nineteen days. The squire hired him to work in his great house in the village. The people in the village laugh at him because he spent all that money so quickly, but he doesn't care. He's happy working for the squire, and he sings in the village church.

I never heard anything more of Long John Silver. That one-legged sailor disappeared from my life. No doubt he is living happily somewhere with his wife and his parrot Captain Flint. I hope he is enjoying this life, because his possibilities of comfort in the next life are very small.

The bars of silver and the guns that Flint had marked on the map are still where he buried them, and they will probably remain there. I know that I will never go back to that terrible island. In my worst dreams, I hear the waves crashing on its beaches, or I hear the voice of Long John's parrot crying, 'Pieces of eight! Pieces of eight!'

Go back to the text

1 Comprehension check
Answer the following questions.

1 How long did it take to carry all the treasure onto the *Hispaniola*?
2 What did they leave for the three remaining pirates?
3 What was the South American port like?
4 How did Long John escape?
5 What did Jim do with his portion of the treasure?
6 What did Ben Gunn do with his?
7 When does Jim think Long John will be punished?
8 When does Jim hear the sound of the sea around Treasure Island?

2 Writing
When *Treasure Island* appeared, many people did not like Long John Silver. They thought that Stevenson made him too interesting and charming for boys. However, Long John Silver became the model for many fictional pirates with his physical disability and his parrot. One of the most famous of these imaginary pirates with a physical disability is Captain Hook. Hook is a character in the book *Peter Pan*, written by Stevenson's friend, J. M. Barrie. In fact, Barrie wrote that Captain Hook was 'the only man that the Sea-Cook feared.' The Sea-Cook is, of course, Long John Silver.
In about 100-150 words give your opinion of Long John Silver. Do you think he is a good character for a children's book?

Include the following information:

• how Long John acts with Jim
• why Long John changes his attitude
• what happens to Long John in the end
• your opinion of Long John's actions
• if you think he is a good character for a children's book

❸ Vocabulary

Find five words in this word spiral related to meals. The remaining letters make three words related to jobs. All eight words appear in this chapter.

Meals

1 meat .... 2 .... 3 .... 4 .... 5 ....

Jobs

1 .... 2 .... 3 ....

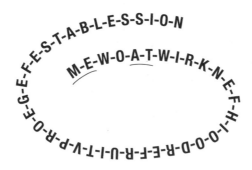

❹ Summary

Put the paragraphs in the right order to make a summary of Chapters Seven-Nine. Then fill in the gaps with the words in the box.

stared	hole	mutineers	shot	pointed	bag	kill
	skeleton	ghost	pile	pirate		

A ☐ When they arrived at the tall tree they found a large
(1) .... The treasure was gone.

B ☐ 1 After capturing the *Hispaniola*, Jim went back to the fort. He
was shocked to find Long John Silver and six (2) ....
Silver told Jim that his friends did not want him back, and so he
had to become a (3) ....

C ☐ The next day Dr Livesey came to help the sick pirates. He
(4) .... at Jim in amazement. Silver let the doctor talk
to Jim. The doctor told Jim that he should run away with him.
Jim said no. The doctor left.

D ☐ Long John, Jim and the pirates then went to look for the tall
tree. The treasure was buried there. As they walked through
the forest they found a (5) .... under a pine tree. It
was in a strange position. Long John understood that it
(6) .... to the treasure.

E ☐ Just then they heard a voice singing the song *Fifteen Men on the
Dead Man's Chest*. The men thought that it was the
(7) .... of Flint and that it wanted to kill them. But
Silver soon realised that it was really Ben Gunn.

F ☐ They took Jim and Silver to Ben Gunn's cave. Here they saw a
large (8) .... of coins and bars of gold.
A few days later they began their voyage home. They left the
three remaining mutineers on the island. They first stopped in
a port in South America. Here Long John Silver escaped with a
(9) .... of coins.

G ☐ They finally arrived safely home, and divided the treasure. Ben
Gunn spent all his in just nineteen days, but the others used
theirs intelligently. Jim knew that there was still some treasure
buried, but he never wanted to return to that terrible
island, and he still heard Long John's parrot crying 'Pieces of
eight!' in his dreams.

H ☐ Jim then told Silver all the things he had done to him. Silver's
men wanted to (10) .... Jim, but Silver stopped them.
They became angry with Silver and gave him the Black Spot. To
save himself, Silver showed the men that he had the treasure
map.

I ☐ Now the pirates were certainly going to kill Jim and Silver.
Silver gave Jim a gun; they were friends again. Just then Jim's
friends appeared and (11) .... two of the pirates.
The other three pirates ran away.

PET **1** Comprehension check

For each question, choose the correct answer — A, B, C or D.

1 Billy Bones gave Jim a silver coin to watch out for
   A ☐ a blind pirate.
   B ☐ a pirate ship.
   C ☐ custom officials.
   D ☐ a pirate with one leg.

2 Pew, the blind pirate, went to see Billy Bones to
   A ☐ ask him for the map.
   B ☐ give him the Black Spot.
   C ☐ kill him and take his gold.
   D ☐ ask him for help against Black Dog.

3 Who had the idea to prepare an expedition to look for the treasure?
   A ☐ Jim
   B ☐ Dr Livesey
   C ☐ Squire Trelawney
   D ☐ Long John Silver

4 Squire Trelawney almost felt proud of the pirate Flint because Flint
   A ☐ fought against many Spanish ships.
   B ☐ had a lot of treasure.
   C ☐ was never caught by the British.
   D ☐ knew how to command dangerous pirates.

5 Who helped the squire find the crew for the *Hispaniola*?
   A ☐ Israel Hands
   B ☐ Dr Livesey
   C ☐ Long John Silver
   D ☐ Jim Hawkins

6 What was Long John Silver's job on the *Hispaniola*?
   A ☐ first mate
   B ☐ captain
   C ☐ cabin boy
   D ☐ cook

7   Who was Ben Gunn?

A ☐   a pirate

B ☐   a British officer

C ☐   a British captain

D ☐   a cook

8   Jim Hawkins helped Israel Hands because

A ☐   Israel had a gun.

B ☐   Israel promised to take him to the treasure.

C ☐   he needed Israel to direct the ship.

D ☐   Jim felt sorry for him.

9   Long John Silver told Jim he should become a pirate because

A ☐   Jim's friends did not want him back again.

B ☐   Jim had killed a man, just like a real pirate.

C ☐   then he could have part of the treasure.

D ☐   Jim had captured a ship, just like a real pirate.

10   Jim's friends gave Long John the treasure map because

A ☐   he promised not to kill them if they gave him the map.

B ☐   they discovered that the map was not real.

C ☐   he promised not to kill Jim if they gave him the map.

D ☐   Ben Gunn had moved the treasure.

11   Ben Gunn pretended that he was the ghost of

A ☐   Captain Flint.

B ☐   Black Dog.

C ☐   Israel Hands.

D ☐   Billy Bones.

12   What did Long John do in the end?

A ☐   He ran away when they were in South America.

B ☐   He ran away when they were back in England.

C ☐   He escaped with Ben Gunn's boat.

D ☐   He stayed with the three pirates on the island.

13   In his bad dreams about his adventure Jim sometimes hears

A ☐   the screams of Allan.

B ☐   the parrot.

C ☐   Ben Gunn's voice.

D ☐   Billy Bones singing 'Fifteen men on the dead man's chest.'

2 Who's Who?

For questions 1-7 say which of the characters from *Treasure Island* is speaking. Choose from the characters in the box. There are three names you do not need to use.

> Jim   Hawkins   Mrs Hawkins   Long John Silver
>
> Dr Livesey   ~~Dick~~   Israel Hands   Pew
>
> Billy Bones   Ben Gunn   Squire Trelawney

When I was just a boy my Mum and Dad told me about the good life, the moral life and the treasure of love. But later friends told me about the good life that comes from the treasure of gold... and I believed them. Oh, what a mistake!

0 ......Dick..

Yes, they were terrible men. They only cared about their gold, their silver, their treasure. Some had swords, some had guns and one had no eyes. But you know something? If somebody owes me money then I will get it. I will even risk my life for that gold and silver. But I am decent person, you know.

1 ....

Come in! Sit down! Are you hungry? Why am I alive now and not dead on that dirty, lonely island of illness? Well, my strength is my intelligence and my words — words like swords and guns. My words tell you that I am your friend and tell you that my sword will not hurt you. Here's a nice apple. Relax, my friend, and tell me about your plans to find that treasure.

2 ....

Well, I lived a difficult life and saw every kind of adventure, and I made many men afraid — afraid of death, afraid of pain... afraid of me! But in the end what killed me? Fear.

3 ....

Yes, my good sir, I am a person of responsibility, of position. People ask my opinion and tell me their private problems and ask me to solve them. I must help them and follow the law. It is an important job indeed, a great obligation to all. For example, a man came to yesterday and told me a secret. Now, listen, this is interesting, he said that...

4 ....

I don't care what you have done. If you are bad, maybe you will go to the gallows or prison. That is right, of course. Maybe you are my enemy, but I will help you. That is my profession and I take my profession seriously, more seriously than your crimes or violence.

5 ....

I have learned many things and seen many things and done many things now. All things were only stories in books for me before, or exciting dreams. I have learned that good actions and kind words can hide cruel intentions. Now I know I can really fight and think like a hero. I can also kill. But I have also learned that there is a price: at night I have frightening visions and sleep often does not bring rest.

6 ....

Yes, I was a bad one, a really bad one — a friend of the cruellest and most dangerous men on the seas — men who kill for gold and silver and jewels. But one day I was suddenly alone, and I soon realised that I really didn't care about their kind of treasures. I discovered that I really liked a certain kind of food, liked it more than gold or silver or jewels.

7

This reader uses the **EXPANSIVE READING** approach, where the text becomes a springboard to improve language skills and to explore historical background, cultural connections and other topics suggested by the text.
The new structures introduced in this step of our READING & TRAINING series are listed below. Naturally, structures from lower steps are included too. For a complete list of structures used over all the six steps, see *The Black Cat Guide to Graded Readers*, which is also downloadable at no cost from our website, blackcat-cideb.com
The vocabulary used at each step is carefully checked against vocabulary lists used for internationally recognised examinations.

Step Three B1.2

All the structures used in the previous levels, plus the following:

Verb tenses
Present Perfect Simple: unfinished past with *for* or *since* (duration form)
Past Perfect Simple: narrative

Verb forms and patterns
Regular verbs and all irregular verbs in current English
Causative: *have / get* + object + past participle
Reported questions and orders with *ask* and *tell*

Modal verbs
Would: hypothesis
Would rather: preference
Should (present and future reference): moral obligation
Ought to (present and future reference): moral obligation
Used to: past habits and states

Types of clause
2nd Conditional: *if* + past, *would(n't)*
Zero, 1st and 2nd conditionals with *unless*
Non-defining relative clauses with *who* and *where*
Clauses of result: *so*; *so ... that*; *such ... that*
Clauses of concession: *although*, *though*

Other
Comparison: *(not) as / so ... as*; *(not) ... enough to*; *too ... to*

Available at Step Three: